THE NEW DIPLOMACY
AND ITS APPARATUS

THE NEW DIPLOMACY
AND ITS APPARATUS

by Geoffrey McDermott

with a foreword by
LORD CHALFONT

The Plume Press Limited
IN ASSOCIATION WITH Ward Lock Limited
116 Baker Street, London W1

First published in 1973 by
the Plume Press Limited
in association with Ward Lock Limited
116 Baker Street, London W1M 2BB
Copyright © Geoffrey McDermott 1973
ISBN 0 7063 1490 5
Printed in Great Britain by
Richard Clay (The Chaucer Press) Ltd
Bungay, Suffolk

Contents

Acknowledgements

I am most grateful to my sternest critic, my son Anthony, for a long list of always constructive suggestions which he has offered, and for sparing the time and energy from his own important journalistic and other writing activities which this operation entailed.

Many thanks are also due to the helpful attitude of political, diplomatic, and journalistic friends too numerous to mention individually; and not least to my contacts in the Foreign and Commonwealth Office, in the United States and Danish embassies in London, and to representatives of the German Democratic Republic both in Berlin and in London.

GEOFFREY MCDERMOTT
July 1972

'In these days there is a great deal of talking and writing about foreign policy, but there can never be too much, since there is an insatiable need for fresh insights and new appraisals.'

George W. Ball,
former US Under-Secretary of State

'Diplomacy is a kind of art of the impossible.'

Lord George-Brown

'I should realize that I have outlived my time. The main underlying forces which must determine British foreign policy have been flowing against the world in which I was born. Nostalgia is not a sound guide to national interest.'

Lord Caccia, Head of H.M. Diplomatic
Service until 1965, speaking in 1972

Foreword

by The Rt. Hon. Lord Chalfont, PC, OBE, MC

One of the many stories told about Ernest Bevin at the Foreign Office describes his first encounter with that unique phenomenon of the Civil Service, the Private Office. About to leave his room on his first Friday evening, the Foreign Secretary discovered on his desk a pile of red boxes; placed neatly and centrally on the top box was a note in the fine Italic hand of the Principal Private Secretary 'The Secretary of State may care to peruse these documents over the weekend'. When the young man arrived at the office on Monday morning he discovered the boxes undisturbed, the note still neat and central on top. Below his polite message was another, in the unmistakably virile scrawl of Mr Bevin. It read quite simply: 'A kindly thought, but erroneous'.

Whether this story is *vero* or just *ben trovato*, it symbolizes one of the decisive moments in the life of a Foreign Office minister—his first encounter with that silky, steely and beautifully articulated machine, the Diplomatic Service. The first trial of strength, which is sometimes no more dramatic than the handshake of two boxers, often decides whether the politician is eventually able to control the machine and use it effectively, or whether he falls into the works and comes out the other end bearing a remarkable resemblance to a rubber stamp. The Foreign Service subscribes collectively to Plato's opinion of politicians, expressed with such timeless precision in the *Republic*: 'When they go to the administration of public affairs, poor and hungering after their own private advantage, thinking that hence they are to snatch the chief good, order there can never be; for they will be fighting about office, and the civil and domestic broils which thus arise will be the ruin of the rulers themselves and of the whole state.' In other words, diplomatists think very little of politicians, believing them in general to be deficient in both virtue and wisdom and quite unfitted to the delicate task of conducting relations with other governments. To the Foreign Service official diplomacy is the proper concern of the philosopher (in the Platonic sense) and not of the placeman.

There is some justification for this rather disobliging view. History—not least contemporary history—is rich with examples of Foreign Secretaries whose defects of temperament, character or intellect have in a few short months reduced years of patient diplomacy to ruins. On the other hand the Foreign Office can sometimes display an infuriating resistance to new ideas in international relations; the memories of *pax Britannica* and an independent British foreign policy, complete with gunboats, *notes verbales*, *bouts de papier* and all the trappings of great power diplomacy, still linger fragrantly in the corridors of Giles Gilbert Scott's elegant but uncomfortable building. It is impossible to work in the atmosphere of the India Office library, the great wall paintings of *Britannia Nutrix* and the gilded splendour of the Secretary of State's vast office, without absorbing at least a little of the traditional conviction that all foreigners secretly long to be British and that, given time and the exercise of discreet diplomacy, they will come round to our way of thinking.

The truth, of course, is that not all politicians are maladroit clowns; and diplomats, in spite of a noticeable penchant for the *status quo*, tend in general to be highly intelligent, patriotic and imaginative. The exceptions usually get found out—sooner or later. The British Foreign Service has a deservedly high reputation in the chancelleries of the world, and it is upon their expertise and industry that the successful day-to-day conduct of our foreign affairs depends. There is, among a few trendy populists, a current theory that the machinery of diplomacy has become superfluous, and that in this century of the common man people should in some unspecified way speak unto people without the intermediacy of governments and their representatives. It is not necessary to take this kind of thing too seriously to accept that the techniques of diplomacy are changing. The remarkable revolution in technology in the twentieth century has changed the whole nature of international relations. The development of the nuclear weapon means that an international crisis might become an international tragedy in a matter of hours, or even minutes. Quick decisions at the highest level are often needed—there is no time for an exchange of stiff notes or of elegantly drafted telegrams. Communications are safe, secure and reliable. Air travel brings heads of governments face to face and 'hot-lines' enable them to speak to each other across the world without rousing ambassadors from their beds. Yet the function of the diplomatic representative is still vital. It is he who must ensure that his government is aware of the shifting patterns of power in the country to which he is accredited; who must provide an accurate assessment of its strengths, its weaknesses and, above all, its intentions—a task too subtle and complex for the most sophisticated of reconnaissance satellites.

As the nature of diplomacy has changed, so has the image of its practitioners. The educational background of the Foreign Office, popularly believed to be exclusively Eton and Magdalen or Winchester and Balliol, is nowadays much more widely based. Something like a third of entrants to the administrative grades (from which the highest posts in the Service are filled) now come from universities other than Oxford and Cambridge. Ten years ago 94 per cent were 'Oxbridge' graduates. Nearly a half of these entrants began their education, not in the glossier public schools but in local education authority-assisted schools. Yet the Foreign Office is not prepared to let a preoccupation with egalitarianism carry it too far. When Mr Michael Stewart was Foreign Secretary he had the bright idea of inviting a group of university vice-chancellors to spend a day at the Foreign Office, discussing with him and his ministers and officials the problem of broadening the academic background of candidates. One of the distinguished visitors was of the opinion that the discussion was based upon a false premise, an undistributed middle and various other logical fallacies. The best brains from any school, he argued, get scholarships to Oxford or Cambridge; so the best candidates are likely to come from those universities, irrespective of their social origins. His conclusion was that to insist upon a wider catchment area implied an acceptance of lower standards. The argument may have weaknesses, but as its advocate was the vice-chancellor of a 'redbrick' university it carried substantial weight in the Foreign Office.

Geoffrey McDermott is, by training and by temperament, admirably suited to the task of analysing some of the changing problems of diplomacy and of opening to public inspection the arcane rituals and practices of the Diplomatic Service. A diplomatist for more than a quarter of a century, he has a wide experience of the Service in all its aspects. He has already raised a few establishment hackles by his public strictures on British intelligence and security—especially in the context of the Philby affair. I confidently predict that this book will raise a few more; but I am equally confident that anyone who reads it will emerge with a deeper understanding of diplomacy and, I dare say, with a higher opinion of diplomatists.

Introduction

My reasons for tackling a book on the new diplomacy and its apparatus are varied. First, it is clear to an ever wider public that diplomacy—and I shall try at a later stage to define that word—is influencing our lives every day of the year; and that a vast apparatus exists—far larger than ever before, and far more complex. The presence of the representatives of over 130 nations at the United Nations is only one example of many. Second, a large number of totally new problems face the diplomat in our fast-moving age, culminating in the question of man's survival under nuclear pressures.

I spent twenty-seven years in His, and later Her, Majesty's Diplomatic Service before retiring with ambassadorial rank at the age of forty-nine. Four successive generations of my family have involved themselves in overseas affairs; who knows whether a fifth, at present one strong and two years old, will not follow suit? I myself was fortunate in that my four last jobs were all concerned not merely with political diplomacy of the traditional kind but also with questions of strategy and intelligence, both of which call for a good deal of forward planning. I have always been more interested in the future than in the past; and while most diplomatic memoirs naturally enough deal with events that have gone before, on my retirement I determined to explore the requirements of diplomacy, in the broadest sense, today and in the future.

I shall try now to answer the sort of questions I am often asked. What are the capabilities of diplomacy? How does the apparatus function? Is it efficient and well adapted to the problems of the 1970s? Looking round the world it would surely be difficult to claim that it is operating very successfully in many places. I shall try to go a little further, in two directions: first, by comparing British methods and approaches with some others;

second, by venturing my own suggestions on how best to cope with the appalling international problems which will face us in the 1970s and 1980s. At the same time, I am well aware that some of my facts and proposals will be out of date by the time this book is published. The international scene changes, sometimes radically, from day to day; and so, to the credit of its operators, does British policy and its diplomatic apparatus.

Although I have inserted my own comments in the course of the narrative, I have deliberately held back some of my major suggestions until the last part of the book. As to style, I have always thought that though many diplomatic matters are of a weighty nature this is no excuse for writing about them pompously or in a desiccated fashion. For what readers is the book intended? Hopefully, as many as possible; to be more specific what I will call, if I may without seeming to condescend, the intelligent layman and by no means least the young—or older—men and women whose ambition it is to become diplomats. If some of those who are already established feel the urge to read it, I shall be more than gratified. As for the apparatus, not merely the British one but those of other nations and, not least, the numerous international bodies, this book must aim to serve a practical purpose if it is not merely to line up with the 'humorous mechanical models', as their originator calls them, of Rowland Emett.

CHAPTER ONE

A New Diplomacy—Why?

The British people as a whole take no intense interest in international affairs. This is natural enough. They have plenty of more immediately pressing matters to concern them: the welfare of their families—covering wages, housing, health services, the environment; and more light-hearted matters such as holidays, the pools and football. And they no longer rule an empire, or rank as a super-power. Foreign trade and commerce, we all understand, are of profound importance to our standard of living; but the general feeling is that their conduct can be left to a relatively small proportion of the population. I believe, however, that in today's world there are dangers in this attitude; and that more interest and responsibility could, and must, be taken by non-experts.

Much the same is true of other peoples in what we broadly call the West; with two exceptions. The United States has involved itself in a grievous war, and very many of its citizens have deep personal reasons for following international developments from day to day. Then in West Germany, which is in fact officially called the Federal Republic of Germany, there are potent personal and political reasons for watching developments in East Germany (properly called the German Democratic Republic) and West Germany's relations with that state. In communist countries in general the potential interest in international affairs is thwarted because there is nothing that the majority of the people can do about them except follow the activities of their leaders. The same applies even more strongly in the numerous developing countries, where simple, and entirely understandable, ignorance of the world scene is bound to play a large part for some time yet.

To take this matter a step further, diplomats, and the tool they use to grapple with international relations, diplomacy, are generally regarded as being highly specialized, esoteric, and privileged. The interest taken in them increases all the time, though the spread is still not broad; but a sort of frustration is apt to set in even among intelligent observers, sometimes culminating in an attitude of disbelief that diplomacy, or diplomats, are really necessary. If they are, why; and what do they achieve; and could they achieve more? Is it not almost incredible that in the Middle East, Asia and Ireland religious wars sometimes of an almost medieval character should be waged towards the end of the twentieth century? Can diplomacy do nothing to prevent them?

These are very pertinent questions, of importance to the future of all of us, and I shall do my best to answer them. Two broad points should be made first. Much misunderstanding is due to the enduring picture in people's minds of the diplomat as a person primarily concerned with protocol, gorgeous uniforms and cocktail parties. There are fewer and fewer of these about today, in the British Diplomatic Service or elsewhere. Secondly, associated with this picture is the idea that diplomacy is and must be a recondite occupation run entirely by experts, and on conventional and traditional lines.

But a good straight look at the world scene today, and its probable developments in the 1970s and beyond, shows that this is not and cannot be the case. One simple answer to the question of whether diplomacy still has an important part to play is that there are now infinitely more diplomats and associated collaborators in the world than there have ever been. The first independent gesture that any newly independent country, however underdeveloped and poor, makes is to send a diplomatic representative to the UN, and others elsewhere if the cost can be afforded. So, to say the least, diplomacy flourishes.

As to the questions: why are diplomats necessary, what do they achieve, and could they achieve more, here briefly are the overriding factors and problems, all of them interlocking, in international relations now and no doubt for ten or twenty years to come. First, with the development of nuclear weapons we possess, for the first time in our history, the power to blow up mankind. Second, there is all the time a constant and rapid increase of armaments of all kinds. This is the case in spite of much talk about disarmament; and the increases in stockpiles are to be seen in the possession not only of the super-powers but also of lesser and even underdeveloped powers to which the arms are peddled. Third, there is the exceedingly dangerous split in the communist world between the USSR and the People's Republic of China, with the latter forging ahead in creating a fourth world dominated by her. Fourth, the proliferation of newly independent countries is unprecedented in the world's history, and there may be another twenty or so to come. Fifth, the gap between richer and poorer countries is constantly widening, in spite of the fact that much lip service is paid to 'aid' in and by the former to the latter. Finally, there is the enormous increase in international bodies, of very varying character and effectiveness.

All of these are elements in the international situation which have been building up since the last world war but which have now reached a stage of such intensity that they present problems on an entirely new level. To take an outstanding example, the relatively simple cold war between the West and Soviet communism is a thing of the past, though there are people in both camps qualified to know better who refuse to admit it. And there is every reason to suppose that these new problems, and others as yet in their infancy, will develop more rather than less rapidly in the coming years. Professor Wedderburn, of the London School of Economics and Political Science, has expressed this view: 'The dominant organization of the next decade will be the multinational or international corporation'; and he quotes a British Cabinet minister who said, in 1968, that national governments, 'including the British government, will be reduced to the status of a parish council in dealing with the large international companies which span the world'.

Consequently, if we want to keep international relations, and in the last resort the world, going along successfully, it is essential to have a new style of diplomacy, if we still care to use that word. Here are the implications, point by point and only briefly at this stage, of the six major factors. The nuclear terror calls for unwavering observation, at every moment, by mechanical intelligence sources as well as by human strategists, scientists and diplomats. The increase in armaments calls for the same. So does the communist split, with emphasis in addition on its trade and aid implications. As for the newly independent countries, they not only have no diplomatic traditions of their own but may justifiably conclude, looking around the world, that the conventional activities of the past have not made a good job of it and that a new approach can only be an improvement. On 'aid', more sincerity, activity and expertise on the part of the richer countries would benefit the world as a whole. Finally, the international bodies have in varying degrees shown that they are not prepared to operate along the lines of the Congress of Vienna. I shall have a good deal more to say on these overriding issues, and others of importance, in my chapter on diplomacy in the 1970s and beyond.

This may appear a gloomy picture. I see it more as a challenge to diplomats and their associates everywhere. Fortunately for their sanity, and that of us members of the general public everywhere, they will not as individuals be occupied with these horrendous problems all, or even most, of the time. There are plenty of day-to-day questions of significance to keep them usefully employed. But the new diplomacy demands that the overriding problems, and the methods of dealing with them, should be in the minds of leaders in all sorts of spheres, of as many of the world's nations as possible, and essentially those of, say, the most powerful dozen nations. I am not for a moment suggesting that we should imitate the—in many ways novel—diplomatic methods of the communist and emerging countries, though no doubt we can learn something from them. I think that we British, the Americans and the West Germans have in fact quite recently begun to practise a new and more effective style of diplomacy.

If I have so far made little mention of the commercial and economic side as such, it is not because I do not appreciate its basic importance but rather because it is no new problem, and also because I shall have comments to make on the propositions in this connection put forward in the Duncan report of 1969 on the British Diplomatic Service. That report itself devoted a section to what it called the 'new diplomacy' which, as I shall try to show, it defined in too narrow and inflexible a manner. Even a mere three years later we can, I think, do better.

CHAPTER TWO

The New Diplomacy in Action

Before attempting to define the nature and capabilities of diplomacy, and in particular of contemporary diplomacy, let us take a look at it in action. Three significant occasions have been Berlin in 1961–62, which I consider a diplomatic success—that is, a success for both the opposing sides involved; the US–British–Soviet negotiations of 1966–67 on Vietnam—a failure; and the Nixon approaches to China and the USSR in 1972, on which it is too early to reach a judgement, though the outlook is very hopeful.

BERLIN

At 8 a.m. on Sunday 13 August 1961 I was woken by a telephone call from a member of my staff in Berlin, who told me that from 2 a.m. heavily armed Vopos, soldiers, and other employees of the East German government had been erecting a barrier along the dividing line between the Soviet sector and the US, British and French sectors. I had taken up my post as British Minister in Berlin only a few weeks before; and it had been obvious that something ominous was in the offing. Not only had Khrushchev been very tough with Kennedy at their meeting in Vienna in June, and delivered yet another ultimatum about recognizing East Germany, but Ulbricht, too, had been on a prolonged visit to Moscow. The whole atmosphere in Berlin was very tense, and refugees had been pouring in across the open frontier between East and West Berlin until they reached the figure of 4,000 in a week, swamping our reception centres.

At 10 a.m. the three Western ministers and commandants, with their staffs, met at the Kommandatura office, with the photograph of the last Soviet officer to attend the 'quadripartite' organization, in 1949, looking sardonically down at us. We formed an unwieldy body, harking back in origin and character to the immediate post-war period and the height of the cold war. The organization is, of course, even more absurd today. On that morning two factors seemed predominant. In the first place, our combined intelligence efforts—including those of the West Berlin senate, or government—had failed to give us any warning of the Wall, in spite of the fact that there was free passage for Berliners between the western and eastern sectors. (This failure must have been largely thanks to George Blake, whose last stamping-ground had been Berlin.) Secondly, we had not had time to get instructions from our various governments.

Consequently we met in a state of great frustration. The discussion followed predictable lines. The us commandant wanted to send his meagre forces to knock the nasty thing down. I pointed out that even if they succeeded temporarily they, plus the even smaller forces of the British and French, could not occupy East Berlin against the infinitely superior East German forces; and that ringed around Berlin were twenty-two Red Army divisions with full air backing, as we knew from the daily sonic booms, while the NATO forces were over a hundred miles distant. Such action by our forces would therefore amount to no more than an escapade, and one with highly dangerous implications; we should have to return with our tails between our legs, and the building of the Wall would be resumed. The French representatives were, as always, logical and cool. So was Lord Mayor Willy Brandt, when we invited him at a later stage to join our confabulations. Meanwhile we had of course already reported the night's happenings by telephone or 'most immediate' telegram to our respective foreign offices, embassies in Bonn, Washington, Paris and Moscow, and to NATO headquarters. After the meeting we reported the rather inconclusive discussions which we had had, and such suggestions for action—in the British case, not military but political and diplomatic—as we could muster. In particular, Brandt sent a personal message through the Americans to his friend President Kennedy, begging him to take what action he could to hold or improve the position. In West Berlin the situation was one of near-panic combines with resigned speculation: what next?

President Kennedy, in consultation with his allies, took several steps. He considered very drastic action, including the use of

nuclear weapons and a type of relief-of-Mafeking advance of
NATO troops through East Germany to Berlin. He wisely turned
these down: they would no doubt have led to a third world war.
In fact the Western reaction was limited, after some forty-eight
hours' consideration, to stiff protests in Moscow to the Soviet
government. This may have seemed feeble to some, but it was
sensible in the long run. Kennedy also ordered a small but significant reinforcement of the US garrison in Berlin. The communists were wise enough to let this pass through their country
without interference. He sent Vice-President Johnson to dis-
tribute ball-point pens and oratory to the West Berliners:
hundreds of thousands turned out to greet him and their morale
was duly boosted. In Washington a group of high-ranking diplomats of the Western allies was set up to meet daily, to co-
ordinate reports from their representatives in Berlin, from the
capitals concerned and from NATO, to obtain decisions on policy
from those in charge and to dispatch these to us in Berlin and to
all concerned elsewhere. As often as not these were conveyed in
cypher telegrams that were both top secret and most immediate;
and, in the form in which they emerged from our cypher
machines, up to a yard long. I remember reflecting, as time
passed, that perhaps there was too much discussion going on in,
particularly, Bonn and Washington. Meanwhile, headquarters at
NATO set up a special contingency planning group on Berlin,
although technically and legally we could not claim NATO's pro-
tection. Finally, Kennedy sent back to Berlin as a sort of super-
commandant a hero of the immediate post-war days, General
Lucius D. Clay. Whether or not his orders were to hot things up
in the city, that is what he did.

The following months were tense indeed. The Wall was
steadily strengthened and made more repulsive. The Vopos
regularly shot men and women trying to cross it. Road traffic
from the West to West Berlin suffered sporadically severe interference. Western civilian aircraft were buzzed, sometimes dangerously. General Clay's breezy policy led to the confrontation
of US and Soviet tanks at a few yards' distance at Checkpoint
Charlie. He quarrelled with both his own and the British commandants and was ordered back home a little later. The French
kept as cool as ever. We continued to get only flimsy intelligence

on the intentions of the East German government. Three more times Kennedy considered seriously whether the situation did not demand a resort to nuclear war. Maudie Littlehampton opined one day that Berlin was becoming a bore and that one good 'nuke' on it might be a blessing.

From time to time the Western allied ambassadors, whom we in Berlin of course kept fully informed on developments every day, came on brief visits to the front-line city, without I think achieving very much. So did a number of politicians. Chancellor Adenauer, who once said that his chief dislikes were 'the Russians, the Prussians and the British', delayed coming as long as possible, and was rude to Brandt—his opponent in the current elections for the chancellorship—when he came. The morale of the West Berliners remained admirably firm.

As the months passed it became increasingly clear to me, and to various observers in political and journalistic circles in the West, though hardly any in West Berlin, that the Wall was here to stay for a long time. Official Western policy of course refused to face this fact. I paid visits to the Soviet commandant and the Soviet embassy in East Berlin, and had reasonably sensible discussions with them. I put some of my ideas to a visiting group of senior members of the Imperial Defence College, as it then was, in May 1962. I was withdrawn from my post in June.

This is not an autobiography, and I will only add in this connection that, thanks to the herculean efforts of Willy Brandt, many of the ideas that I put forward in the press, in 1962 and subsequently, are now approaching fruition, ten years later. But my main point is that over Berlin in 1961–62, and of course later as tension bit by bit subsided, the new diplomacy could be seen at work. There was never time for leisurely consultations, or for the proper forms to be observed. A crisis which led to the brink was deliberately fostered, in a most aggressive way, by the communists, for two basic reasons. First, they judged that the Wall was essential to their security and prosperity. They judged right. Second, they judged that the West would be sensible enough not to cross the brink. Here again they judged right, by a whisker. On the Western side, too, our diplomacy was of a new kind. Not only did big decisions have to be taken at high speed; they had to cover a multiplicity of interests, which had different weight for each of the allies, and a great variety of people outside the official diplomats contributed to them. Possibly the most important new factor was Kennedy's use of a group of what were considered 'liberal' intellectuals, appointed by him personally, to advise him at every turn. This was a different matter from the appointment of Dean Rusk as Secretary of State, or Robert McNamara as Secretary of Defense. In any case Kennedy paid little attention to the views of the State Department, which he regarded as 'a bowlful of jelly'. The able Professor J. K. Galbraith, Kennedy's ambassador to India, held similar views. 'The State Department convened a meeting in London to talk about the Kashmir talks. Those attending talked for some twenty hours and agreed on doing what was already being done. I got a long and elaborate and meaningless telegram which said I should do what I had told them I was already doing.

'Note: These meetings of middle-level officials, held in great solemnity, are among the world's more ceremonious boondoggles.' (Ah! How well I remember those boondoggles!)

But the Bundys and the Rostows had Kennedy's ear at any time of day or night. Over Berlin their advice was sound; so it was over the Cuba missile crisis later in 1962. Over Vietnam it was disastrous; and we shall see it at work in the next illustration of the new diplomacy in action.

I said earlier that I considered the Berlin affair a success for both sides; and this should be the objective of diplomacy, certainly in critical cases. If either had gone too far, both would have failed. The West may have lost a little face in the short run, but this is hardly a major consideration since in the longer run the new arrangements in Berlin contributed materially to a great easing of tension, not only there but in East–West relations generally.

VIETNAM

One of the most balanced advisers summoned by Kennedy to serve in the White House was Chester Cooper, a long-established member of the CIA and a true expert on Vietnam, who had proved a highly successful and popular liaison officer in London with the British intelligence community in the 1950s. He struggled consistently to dissuade Kennedy from the escalation of us interference in Vietnam; and he was consistently overruled. Under President Johnson it soon became clear to him that the struggle was hopeless, and he quit the White House.

Cooper has described vividly the hit-and-miss methods used by Johnson in prosecuting the war, and in holding the diplomatic ring while he pressed ahead in accordance with the wishes of the military–industrial complex, with which people like McNamara and the 'liberal' intellectuals were happy to agree. Three examples of Johnson's methods which directly involved the British government are pertinent here.

On 27 December 1965 Johnson telephoned Washington from his Texas ranch to ask when the pause in bombing North Vietnam was due to end. It seems extraordinary that he did not have the information already. However, the two Bundy brothers hustled off from some party, in white tie and tails, to the State Department, and later communicated the information to the President. On the advice of Cooper and one or two other sensible people the President ordered that the pause should be extended, though only slightly. Johnson now thought it appropriate to despatch important figures like Averell Harriman and Hubert Humphrey to Europe and Asia for the purpose of explaining how magnanimous he was being. The Hanoi reaction was to describe them as 'freaks and monsters'. Cooper had meanwhile recommended that Prime Minister Harold Wilson, with whom he had been on friendly terms for some years, might be able to do some useful bridging work in Moscow when he went there on 21 February 1966. Johnson made clear what he thought of that proposition by ordering the resumption of the bombing shortly before Wilson's visit. Wilson at this stage publicly expressed disapproval of the bombing, none too soon and ineffectually into the bargain; this gesture did not endear him to Johnson. The President, for the sake of his image, now appointed Harriman his ambassador-at-large 'in charge of peace'. Cooper had had enough of the White House, and agreed to become Harriman's one and only aide.

That episode was a diplomatic fiasco, and another was to follow. In his new capacity Cooper discussed Vietnam with Wilson and Foreign Secretary George Brown in London in November 1966. Nothing daunted by Wilson's experience,

Brown was confident that he could persuade the Soviet government 'to inch Hanoi towards negotiations' when he visited Moscow later that month. Cooper was sceptical; the British, he thought, had been 'especially active and singularly unsuccessful' in trying to establish contacts with Hanoi. However, Brown tried it on. He indicated to the Soviet government that he had authority from his 'friends in Washington' to put forward a de-escalation formula called Phase A–Phase B, of which more in a moment. What his friends had not told him was that the formula had previously been given secretly to a Polish intermediary, so that the Soviet government was already aware of it. On learning this Brown was, naturally, furious.

Wilson and Brown were still not dismayed, though they might have been if they had known that Johnson and some of his top advisers 'took a rather dim view of Wilson's eagerness to discuss Vietnam with Kosygin'. The Soviet Premier was due in London on 6 February 1967, and Wilson asked that Cooper should come to London on 3 February to give him an up-to-the-minute briefing on US policy on Vietnam. At Wilson's request he was to stay throughout the visit to act as a link with Washington if required. Given the existence of the Foreign Office, the State Department, the US embassy in London and the British embassy in Washington, not to mention the No. 10 to White House hot-line, this was a novel style of diplomacy. Wilson tactlessly asked Cooper for a blanket commitment that the US government would in future tell the British government everything about Vietnam, however sensitive. Cooper of course had to refuse.

Wilson opened discussions with Kosygin by proposing, as had so often been done fruitlessly in the past, that the Geneva Conference should be reconvened. That was turned down flat by all concerned—Washington, Moscow, Peking, Hanoi. But when Wilson mentioned a Phase A–Phase B formula Kosygin displayed interest and asked to have it in writing. The US government asked Wilson to put it like this: Phase A—the bombing of North Vietnam will stop; Phase B—the infiltration of North Vietnamese troops, and also the increase of American troops, will both stop. Two Foreign Office officials and Cooper then drafted a paper to be handed to Kosygin, on the lines the State Department had prescribed. Cooper cabled the draft statement through the US embassy in London to Washington, 'confident that it required little more than proforma approval'.

By the evening of the next day, when Washington had had ample time to reply if they were taking the matter seriously, no answer had been received. All concerned in London took no news as being good news, and Kosygin was given his piece of paper, which he was to study on a trip to Scotland. Cooper, with a sigh of relief, went off to see *Fiddler on the Roof*. Not for long: he was called to a telephone near the stage door, and Walt Rostow, on the line from the White House, told him to 'get back damn fast' to the US embassy. From there Rostow ordered him off to 10 Downing Street, where the authorized message to be given to Kosygin would arrive over the hot-line.

It came immediately; and in Cooper's words 'we were in a brand-new ball-game'. In effect it was Phase A–Phase B turned upside down. Hanoi were called on to stop infiltration first. Cooper had high words with Rostow across the Atlantic, but to no avail: the President had made up his mind. Wilson and Brown felt frustrated, to put it mildly. Wilson called the White House and explained, with elaborate self-control, how damaging it all was. A private secretary rushed the new message round to Kosygin just as he was boarding his train for Scotland.

Two days later Kosygin, Wilson, Brown, Cooper and others had Sunday lunch at Chequers. Kosygin never mentioned the switch of notes. After midnight, back at No. 10, a further message arrived from Washington. If the North Vietnamese troops north of the 17th parallel stood fast, the existing bombing pause would be extended. But Hanoi must give its assurances by 10 a.m. the next day, Monday. This was, of course, an impossible deadline. Kosygin obligingly promised to do what he could. US Ambassador Bruce rang Secretary of State Rusk and urged him to be reasonable. Rusk replied that 'the British had been given all they were going to get', and that Bruce must not bother him again. Hanoi did not reply. On the Monday afternoon the bombing began again. And so, comments Cooper, 'the peace efforts from November through mid-February ended in another pall of smoke over Hanoi'.

These episodes illustrate the new diplomacy at its worst. It would be fair to call them examples of spasm diplomacy.

Obviously Johnson, together with the military–industrial complex represented by McNamara and General Westmoreland, and 'respectable' intellectual advisers like the Rostows and the Bundys, had no serious intention of reaching agreement with Hanoi, and made this crudely clear. The officials of the State Department and the Foreign Office were not asked to play any active part. Purely for the record Johnson allowed Cooper to try to bring Kosygin, Wilson and Brown into a 'peacemaking' ploy. The President clearly had no real faith in the efforts of any of them. Obviously Kosygin, with the two contrasting messages in his hands, realized that the whole exercise was nugatory. He might have reacted much more adversely than he did. Wilson told MPs and the press that 'peace was in his grasp': a supreme example of euphoria. The 'special relationship' between Britain and the United States was yet again proved to be by no means as special as in the past, and the hot-line to be merely tepid compared with the only real hot-line, that between Washington and Moscow. The North Vietnamese government, for its part, was never likely to be impressed by what amounted to an ultimatum on the lines that unless they met Johnson's conditions, and fast, the process of 'bombing them back into the Stone Age' would continue. And so the Kennedy–McNamara–Johnson war dragged on in 1972.

THE UNITED STATES, CHINA AND THE SOVIET UNION

As early as 1961 it was being freely acknowledged in circles close to President Kennedy that the People's Republic of China should be fully recognized for what she was, one of the world's superpowers. Two principal factors accounted for the delay of ten years before this view could be translated into reality. One was the ridiculously misnamed 'cultural revolution' inside China, which was in fact a profound upheaval that involved the Chinese government and people in a long succession of political, diplomatic and personal acts of violence of an untypically uncivilized character. On the other side, it was impossible for a Democrat President to flout the China—really anti-China—lobby and provoke the accusation of being 'soft on communism', particularly when it was Chinese communism temporarily on the rampage.

President Nixon inherited a fearful legacy when he took over in January 1969. Worst of all were the problems at home: the deep social disruption at many levels—a 'cultural revolution' included—and the increasingly creaking economy. Intimately connected with these, it was essential that the Vietnam war should be wound down, and eventually wound up. The President also reckoned that any novel diplomatic initiatives, particularly in connection with the communist world, could bring in a useful bonus. He, and his Vice-President, Spiro Agnew, were after all in no danger of being accused of crypto-communism.

President Nixon approached his diplomatic problems from two angles. He showed no greater confidence in the State Department and the US Foreign Service than had his predecessors. He appointed an agreeable nonentity, William Rogers, as Secretary of State. In accordance with American tradition, he rewarded faithful party supporters, many of them with absolutely no claims to diplomatic expertise, with plum ambassadorial jobs, Walter Annenberg in London being a case in point.

But at the same time he stepped up the unconventional sides of American diplomacy. The head of the CIA, Richard Helms, was ordered to sharpen up the Agency and its operations. Above all, a personal 'special security adviser', in the shape of Dr Henry Kissinger, was installed in the White House with a large staff, with access to all information and advice from the CIA and the State Department—and some not vouchsafed even to them—and, finally, with immediate access, day and night, to the President. This remarkable man is in his forties, was born German and Jewish, and escaped to the US in 1938 when he was fifteen. Thus the White House super-think-tank was set up.

The President set about assuring his allies all over the world that the United States would remain faithful to them, though the American military forces in Vietnam were to be steadily and drastically reduced. He was conciliatory towards the USSR, and encouraged Willy Brandt in his sterling efforts towards *détente* in Europe. But he wanted something more. Frankly, he wanted to bring off some coup that would reinforce his chances of re-election in 1972. The scene at home, covering the whole spectrum from racial troubles to the decline of the dollar, was not encouraging. He asked Kissinger to think up some diplomatic ploy of a sensational kind—the more outrageous the better.

Kissinger had to work out the balance between an enormous number of conflicting, or at the least overlapping, interests. There was Congress, with all its variety of views and prejudices. There were the State Department and the CIA. There were the Defense Department and the Pentagon, heavily backed by the military–industrial complex. There were the gigantic US-controlled international corporations and trading concerns. There were the American allies and clients, including such powerful nations as Japan. There were also her enemies to be considered. Eventually he came up with about the most far-out idea conceivable: not only should the US government abandon Taiwan and support the entry of communist China into the United Nations; not only should the hand of friendship be extended in general to China; but the President himself should go and visit in his lair Mao Tse-tung, the patron saint of all that is most un-American in the world.

The plan called for secret diplomacy of the most elaborate kind. Naturally the State Department was not consulted; only an extremely small number of its members were even informed. More naturally still, even the US's closest allies could not be informed in advance. Kissinger himself contrived to make two visits to China without being detected. If the KGB had any inkling of what was going on, it reckoned it best to reveal nothing. And so in due course communist China replaced Taiwan in both the Security Council and the General Assembly of the UN; and, comically, in November 1971 Dr Kissinger's curly-haired ten-year-old son blurted out in the President's aircraft, which was crammed with journalists, that Mr Nixon would visit China in March 1972. He was wrong, but only by a few days.

Just before the President's arrival in China on 21 February 1972, George Kennan, one of the US's best diplomats and now retired, had this to say about the visit. 'It flies in the face of all professional diplomatic experience, which suggests that meetings at the summit, if they are to have value at all, should take place only after outstanding political questions have been successfully treated at the normal diplomatic level.' With all respect to the Professor, as he now is, I think this judgement shows he is out of touch with diplomatic methods today. On the negative side, Khrushchev's destruction of the Paris summit meeting because he had lost his temper over the U2 incident shows how the most meticulously prepared diplomatic encounter can come to nothing for extraneous causes. Secondly, Professor Kennan himself puts the positive side well: 'What better stance for Mr Nixon than that of the bold world statesman, taking imaginative and dramatic action in the cause of peace, sweeping aside the sterile rigidities of the cold war.'

And this is exactly what the visit proved. Chairman Mao received President Nixon, and they talked amicably. At the state banquet on 21 February the President explained lucidly what the visit could achieve, and what it could not. 'What we say here will not be long remembered. What we do here can change the world. . . . If in the future we can find common ground to work together, the chances for world peace are immeasurably increased. . . . Neither of us seeks to stretch out our hands and rule the world.' And before finally proposing the toast to friendship, the President slipped in a graceful tribute: 'Chairman Mao has written: "So many deeds cry out to be done, and always urgently. The world rolls on. Time passes. Ten thousand years are too long. Seize the day. Seize the hour." ' The final communiqué, issued at the end of the week's visit, confirmed what the President had already made clear in connection with the UN question: that there is only one China, that Taiwan is part of it, and that the Taiwan question should be resolved 'by the Chinese themselves'. In return the Chinese government undertook to 'facilitate' bilateral exchanges in the spheres of trade, science, technology, culture, sport, and so on. It was implied that a gradual approach towards normal diplomatic relations would take place. At a farewell banquet the President said: 'This was the week we changed the world. Generations in the years ahead will look back and thank us for this meeting.'

It is easy to be cynical about the whole affair; but while cynicism has a considerable part to play in diplomacy, it is hardly constructive in itself. The final communiqué largely catalogued the issues on which the two sides agreed to differ; but this is better than papering over cracks. Also it ended on a positive note about future Sino-American relations.

Another cynical comment might be that jamborees of this kind create more problems than they solve. Certainly the new problems are formidable. All the US's Asian friends and allies took fright in varying degrees; probably worst of all the South Vietnamese and the Japanese.[1] The USSR was deeply disturbed and would have to be placated. The war in Vietnam was shortly afterwards escalated by Hanoi; Nixon decided to riposte by heavy bombing of the North. The attitude of Maoists throughout the world was ambivalent, some regarding the meetings as a great success for their cause, others as a betrayal of it. A final irony: when Dom Mintoff of Malta arrived in China a few weeks later he was treated to an official banquet on exactly the same scale as President Nixon had been; he received a tumultuous welcome from a crowd of about 100,000; and he was promised help to make Malta independent of the British military base.

By now it was apparent to the governments of both North and South Vietnam that they were going to be treated more than ever as pawns in the super-power game by their respective patrons. The Chinese government egged on the North Vietnamese to launch a big attack, with the double object of embarrassing the Americans in their withdrawal and provoking them into counter-action so violent that the Soviet government would be forced to cancel President Nixon's visit. Here again the mercurial Dr Kissinger played his part. He went off secretly to Moscow where, as always in his unique case, protocol was waived and he was received by the top men. He told them that the President was forced to hit back hard in Vietnam; he refused to say just how. He indicated that the latest North Vietnamese attacks were a deliberate Chinese provocation aimed at ruining the most important diplomatic prospect in the world, that of US–Soviet *rapprochement*. He begged the Soviet leaders not to be

---

[1] The resumption, after thirty-five years, of diplomatic relations between China and Japan, is a measure of this shock.

provoked: could they not either call their North Vietnamese clients off, or simply leave them to their own devices?

Kissinger was able to report to the President that the Soviet government had its priorities right. In particular, in connection with the Strategic Arms Limitation Talks, it had made up its mind that more than enough in the nuclear sphere, on both sides, was more than enough. So the President astonished the world by mining the North Vietnamese harbours and launching an extremely heavy and prolonged aerial bombing attack on North Vietnam. These measures produced the expected protests from all over the world; but those from both China and the USSR were clearly made just for the record. Large numbers of politicians and journalists everywhere speculated, often with *Schadenfreude*, that the Moscow summit was surely off. But no cancellation came; and a few days before the President's departure was due a Soviet minister visiting him in Washington asked: 'Whoever talked about cancellation?'

The President duly took off on time, on 20 May; while the mines remained active and the bombing continued. He was accompanied by his wife, by Dr Kissinger of course, by Secretary of State William Rogers, a staff of thirty-six, and 260 journalists. 'This summit,' he said, 'is primarily directed towards substance, not cosmetics.' The results are well known, and can fairly be called epoch-making. First and best of all were the measures agreed on the limitation of strategic, that is to say thermo-nuclear, armaments: this was only finalized on the plane bringing the chief American and Soviet SALT negotiators from Helsinki to meet the President in Moscow. A long list of subjects on which co-operation was agreed included commerce, science and technology, space, and *détente* both in Europe and even in the Middle East on the basis of the Security Council's Resolution 242. On Indo-China they agreed to differ.

In all, the joint US–Soviet communiqué included thirteen major headings. The shorter joint declaration on 'basic principles of relations between the USA and the USSR' summarized the principal ways in which the two countries could work together to ensure the peaceful solution of all problems. Its two final paragraphs read: '11. The USA and the USSR make no claims for themselves, and would not recognize the claims of anyone else, to any special rights or advantages in world affairs. They recognize the sovereign equality of all states. The development of US–Soviet relations is not directed against third countries and their interests. 12. The basic principles set forth in this document do not affect any obligations with respect to other countries earlier assumed by the USA and the USSR.'

The President's visit was acclaimed in the USSR as an enormous personal, as well as diplomatic, success. Mr Nixon gave sport-loving Leonid Brezhnev a huge Cadillac to add to his stable, which included a modest Citröen-Maserati from President Pompidou and a Rolls-Royce certainly not donated by Mr Heath or Sir Alec Douglas-Home. He repeated the success during his brief visit to Warsaw. A few days later Dr Kissinger went to Tokyo with the fiendishly difficult assignment of placating the Japanese government. And, no more than a couple of weeks later, back he goes to Peking with a good deal of explaining to do. Next, we learnt that he was in touch with those who count in Hanoi. Dr Kissinger is surely the most hard-working—and successful—itinerant diplomat in history. The Soviet government simultaneously carried out its part of the bargain by sending President Podgorny on a peace mission to Hanoi. And shortly afterwards even blood-and-thunder Kim Il Sung of North Korea was making peaceful noises to his Seoul compatriots. Even in the Middle East startling, and promising, side-effects followed in July. Nixon and Kissinger knew before they went to Moscow that the Russians were growing increasingly unpopular in Egypt, for two main reasons. One was their colonialist attitude; for example, President Sadat himself was on one occasion denied access to the Soviet naval base at Mersa Matruh, on Egyptian soil. Second, he is a devout Moslem, as are his richest Arab backers, King Feisal and President Gaddafi of Libya, and communist atheism is anathema to him. Soviet–US agreement on merely mentioning Resolution 242 on the Middle East appeared to Sadat as collusion of a most unsatisfactory kind from the Egyptian point of view. So, cutting off his nose to spite his face, he expelled large numbers of Soviet advisers, instructors, and experts generally; and they took much of their most sophisticated weaponry with them. The Soviet–Egyptian link is likely to remain, in weakened form. But undoubtedly some Egyptian–Israeli peace contacts are going on behind the scenes, and Ambassador Jarring was soon on the prowl again. It seems likely that President Nixon, as his part of the bargain, is urging the Israelis to be more reasonable and to move nearer to the spirit of Resolution 242. President Sadat is a weak character, and as such is liable to lash out in a militarily masochistic fashion; but if he can only resist the temptation, the prospects of some peace settlement, instead of the frustrating 'no peace, no war' situation, now look decidedly brighter.

There were of course many who doubted the value of the Moscow operation. The hard-line right-wingers in the US, and in countries such as Britain, who regard tension as an essential fact of life and prefer the threat of war to the threat of peace, predictably raised their voices. Defense Secretary Melvin Laird immediately declared that the limitation on ICBMs (intercontinental ballistic missiles) would actually call for additional expenditure of some billions of dollars on extra-sophisticated offensive weaponry. The Chinese government appeared stunned into silence: its attack on the US did not come until mid-June, and even then it only consisted of some routine vituperation about Vietnam by the Chinese representative to the slightly ridiculous conference on the environment in Stockholm. The British government welcomed the President's achievements in customary lukewarm manner, and emphasized the difficulties which lay ahead.

But in fact life will never be the same again for the cold warriors of the world. The President and Kissinger had judged accurately the balance of the Soviet government's thinking which, with apologies to Andrew Marvell, might be expressed thus:

> *But at my back I always hear*
> *Nuclear China clattering near;*
> *And yonder all before us lie*
> *Deserts, of vast eternity. . . .*
> *The grave's a fine and private place;*
> *But none I think do there embrace.*

Washington now has better relations with both Moscow and

Peking than they have with each other. As a result of daringly unconventional thinking, sophisticated use of a very special messenger, and meticulous preparation over many months, President Nixon achieved remarkable diplomatic successes in an original manner when they could not possibly have been achieved by 'normal', or in other words old-fashioned, diplomatic methods. He set his sights very high, yet not too high. Thus in his report to Congress after Moscow he said that his trip was 'the beginning of a process that can lead to a lasting peace. The threat of war has not been eliminated. It has been reduced.' Vietnam was 'one of the most extensively discussed subjects', but he declined to give details: hopeful signs on both counts. Shall we see him next in Hanoi? Without being a great admirer of Nixon overall, I have the utmost admiration for his courageous new-style diplomacy. It would not be too fanciful to suggest that he should take his place in the list of Nobel peace prize-winners.[1]

It is too soon to attempt as yet to gauge the long-term effects of this complex of visits. My own view is that the President's farewell remarks in Peking, even if somewhat grandiloquently expressed, may well prove justified. Let us hope so. But whether they do or not there is no doubt that these striking initiatives illustrate the novel features of a completely new style and method of diplomacy, which we can applaud because its object is not to preserve an unsatisfactory *status quo*, nor a dangerous stagnation; but peace. There is therefore every reason why this new diplomacy—flexible, dynamic, even provocative, but with the risks as deeply calculated and weighed as is humanly possible—should be applied to international problems both great and small in the future. Some may say that these were the brinkmanship methods used by the USSR in the 1950s and 1960s, which caused so much tension on so many fronts. The answer is that, first, they led to no major catastrophe and, objectively observed, served the Soviet bloc very satisfactorily throughout when they felt themselves to be in a threatened situation, and second, and more important, the problems in the 1970s are and will be basically

---

[1] Six months later he was officially proposed for the prize. But in between he threw in the December B52 saturation bombing.

different. Whatever some people in both the West and the East may consciously or subconsciously wish, the cold war in its old form is over. It is time for diplomacy to pass from a defensive to a constructive phase. It is high time for the West, and for the Soviet bloc, too, to take initiatives, even risky initiatives.

CHAPTER THREE

The Nature and Capabilities of Diplomacy

SOME DEFINITIONS

Having looked at some concrete examples of diplomacy in action, it is worth trying to define its nature and its capabilities—and its limitations.

A well-known definition was offered by Sir Henry Wotton, an ambassador sent into the field by King James I, who described his job as that of 'an honest man sent abroad to lie for the good of his country'. This statement is subject to two interpretations beyond the obvious one. 'To lie' can also mean 'to live'; and in the case of the British ambassador to the insatiable Catherine the Great it meant something more strenuous again. One dictionary definition of 'diplomatic' gives 'uncandid'; of 'diplomacy', 'tact'; and of 'diplomat', an 'adroit negotiator'. One facetious comment has been that diplomacy is the art of letting the other side have your own way. Balzac considered it 'the science of those who possess no other and who are profound in their vacuity; a convenient science in that it fulfils itself merely in its exercise; a science which permits its practitioners to say nothing and shelter behind mysterious nods of the head; a science, finally, whose most successful exponent is he who can swim with his head above the stream of events he pretends to conduct.' Proust put it slightly differently. His diplomat 'in the course of a long career of diplomacy had become imbued with that negative, methodical, conservative spirit called governmental, which is common to all governments and, under every government, particularly inspires its Foreign Office'. (As we have since 1970 had a Foreign Secretary who is constantly *à la recherche de temps perdu*, this may be particularly appropriate.)

Lord Curzon's comment on diplomatic method was half sensible, half silly. He rightly remarked that the good diplomat will first make up his mind on what his objectives are. But he went on to add that he will also make sure that the people on the other side with whom he is dealing are equally aware of those objectives. In many cases, however, this would be fatally inhibiting to negotiations and relations; eventually of course it should be the case, but it is a question of taking matters step by step, sometimes of using a little subtlety and deception—in fact a matter of timing. In addition, Curzon's is an old-fashioned and one-sided approach to diplomacy. Now and in the future it is at least equally important to know, in respect of the people with whom you are dealing, whether friends or foes, as much as possible about their real capabilities as regards the matters in hand; their own estimate of those capabilities, which may be very different; and their estimate of your capabilities, to be compared with your own estimate. It is because insufficient trouble is taken over all these processes that diplomacy frequently proves inadequate.

The general impression conveyed by such definitions is that diplomacy is something esoteric, a sort of game with serious overtones to be played by craftily-trained gentlemen, preferably noble or upper-class and rich, and of course prepared to bend the truth. The Italians, well educated by Machiavelli, flourished in this type of diplomacy. But the past masters were the French, and the signs of their supremacy contribute even today to making diplomacy seem an arcane science. Thus, contrary to the literal translation of the term *note verbale*, such a communication has for long been, in diplomatic usage, one of the highest formality; the English 'note' seems equally absurd for the purpose. A less formal communication is an *aide-mémoire*; as the plural is the same as the singular in French most non-French diplomats cavalierly use the invention *aides-mémoires* when they feel like it. Less formal still is *un bout de papier*, which would sound frivolous as 'a scrap of paper'. Again, when an ambassador is absent from his post his work is done not by a 'deputy ambassador'—except, to their credit, in the US Foreign Service—but by a *chargé d'affaires*, a cumbrous term. Although English is now used much more for these formalities than in even the recent past, the number of gallicisms in diplomatic parlance is still virtually endless: *laisser-passer, détente, démenti,* and so on. When a foreign government is asked to approve the proposed appointment of a new ambassador it is requested to give not its 'agreement' but its *agrément.* In one of my posts it was even customary to use the bastard term *note non-officielle.*

THE CONTEMPORARY SCENE

Although Britain has produced and still produces a number of diplomats of high quality, our forte until recent times has rather been trade, military action in the broadest sense, and the governing of foreign countries. Even our balancing act in Europe in the nineteenth and early twentieth centuries basically depended on the first two of these elements. Now we are relatively weaker than several countries in the economic and military spheres, and absolutely weaker than the two super-powers; and the Empire has gone for ever. This suggests that, if we are to maintain anything like our present position in the world, diplomacy can play a more significant part than in the past, always subject to the essential condition that our methods are kept strictly up to date and indeed forward-looking.

First, we need a more contemporary definition of diplomacy and its objectives than those mentioned above. 'Dining is the soul of diplomacy', said Lord Palmerston. As diplomacy today has no soul and is more akin to business, we can and should put less emphasis on the dining. It is also wise not to speak of morality in connection with diplomacy. The strong tendency in Western countries is to talk and write as if Christian morality were, if not the only serious type, at least the best in the world. But this view is simply not accepted by half the world's inhabitants, who hold just as strongly that the best moral system is either atheist, or Buddhist, or Hindu, or Moslem, or something else. The good diplomat will avoid an attitude of moral superiority, for it will only hamper the effectiveness of his diplomacy. A fair definition today is that diplomacy is concerned with the management of international relations. Every state, whatever its calibre and size, wants to maintain or improve its position in the world. That is a fact; though it is also a fact that the world would be better off with far fewer nationally-minded states. However, for this actual purpose it is necessary for governments and peoples to know what others are thinking and doing.

A DIPLOMAT'S DUTIES

Mr Harold Macmillan gives his definition in his preface to Sir Charles Johnston's book, *The Brink of Jordan*, about his embassy to that country from 1956 to 1960. 'A British ambassador's function is not, as many people believe, to act as a mere mechanism for the transmission of messages from the home government. There are many posts where the character and personality of our ambassador may still be decisive. He has a double task: he must be able, by consistent, firm and concise messages, to present his case and even impose his will on both sides of Downing Street. He must also have the power to become a trusted friend and adviser of the government to which he is accredited, which in a true sense it is his business not only to advise but to sustain.' Johnston himself, an admirably dynamic ambassador in Amman, puts it rather differently: 'In fact Amman is the ideal post, and will certainly spoil us for conventional ones later on—a real job to be done (very rare in our line of business).' Mr Macmillan's description applied aptly enough to diplomacy in, say, the 1930s, 1940s, and part of the 1950s, and pinpoints some of the qualities that are always desirable in a good top diplomat; but it does not get to the heart of the matter as far as the 1970s are concerned.

The diplomat's duty today and tomorrow is much more like that of a manager (ambassador), sub-manager or member of the staff of a gigantic international corporation, except that he is not in the business for personal profit. The skills that he is called upon to possess and develop must be aimed in that direction. His first duty is to observe, report, and comment accurately on the sphere of foreign affairs entrusted to him. This applies equally in the field and in the Foreign and Commonwealth Office. If someone comments that this is not very glamorous diplomacy, my reply is that diplomacy today must forget all about glamour and deal with brass tacks instead. The diplomat's next duty is to make friends and influence people, including as far as possible those who are not friendly. In the case of Britain our situation demands that our diplomacy should work to bring about and maintain peace. This means, very importantly, we should also recognize that there are governments, and millions of people in the world, who want not peace but war. The Soviet government has taken care so far not to get involved in war since 1945, but readily uses other nations' wars as an instrument of policy. The US government has been far less prudent, and has got its country heavily involved as a result on several occasions. Some Arab governments, such as those of Egypt, Jordan and Syria, involve their peoples in war with zest. The same goes for the Vietnamese and Korean Democratic Republics. Others will follow sooner or later, the most dangerous possibility being China. There is little that British diplomacy can do today to curb any of these warlike policies. But any euphoria, failure to observe and report on them correctly, or inaccurate judgements on their implications, could land us in serious trouble.

A little more about this fundamental question of reporting. I by no means intend to imply that reporting on the dangers of war is for most of the time the only, or even the most important, duty of the British diplomat. I shall try to define our priorities later. There is an inclination even today on the part of some British diplomats to glance down their noses at journalists, though the relationship is distinctly better than it used to be. Most diplomats of that stamp would in fact be of my generation, and so on the point of retirement. The improvement is typified by the fact that a young leader-writer on diplomatic affairs can today without difficulty have an hour's discussion with an assistant under-secretary when a topic is burning. This profitable type of relationship must of course develop from trust on both sides. The FCO would not, for instance, look askance at a journalist maintaining contact even with apparently dubious characters in, say, some communist embassies, though they would welcome some report on what such a contact might produce.

From my experience of both professions I would say that good journalists are at least as efficient reporters as good diplomats; sometimes better, sometimes not. Some editors may evaluate their reports less than objectively; but they will not often do so deliberately in a way designed to harm British interests, though slants in certain papers, such as that towards nostalgia for the

Empire, or an old-fashioned attitude towards foreigners as such, can be injurious. And the FCO evaluators for their part have to deal with widely differing policies from the politicians of the two rival parties: think of Rhodesia, the supply of arms to the Union of South Africa, the United Nations and several other crucial issues. I know from the best possible sources—and what point is there in being mealy-mouthed about this?—that several FCO ministers (there were a baker's dozen of them in all) during the nearly six years of the Labour government felt strongly that the whole weight of our diplomatic apparatus was leaning against any changes of direction in our foreign policy. Lord Chalfont, for one, observed how skilfully the professional diplomats coped with the different sorts of new-type minister: the quasi-official, the typical trade unionist, the ebullient extrovert, the ex-colonial governor who had seen the light. The quasi-official, such as Gordon Walker or Stewart, becomes *plus F.O. que le F.O.*, in Cabinet for instance; just as some elderly ambassadors work on the lines of 'my (foreign) country right or wrong'.

This pinpoints one of the official's dilemmas. If diplomats, however senior or junior, are the permanent staff of this great corporation, they have a board of directors above them, in the shape of ministers, to decide policy; and a mass of shareholders, less intimately concerned with the day-to-day running of the business but entitled none the less to intervene at will, in the shape of Parliament. If the professional diplomat disagrees whole-heartedly with some new policy, he can resign. This is rare: a couple of junior diplomats did so over Suez in 1956, while a considerable number of seniors contented themselves with grumbling. Or he can continue his submissions advocating the same policy as before, which will probably result in his being hustled off to some unattractive post. Or again he can, by subtly modulating the emphasis of the different factors in the case, do as he is told. One of our ablest and least stuffy diplomats—grade two at the age of forty-nine—told me that he had found no difficulty in being the diplomatic private secretary at No. 10 to both Alec Douglas-Home and Harold Wilson. This finally proves what a good diplomat he is. In general, such is the life of a diplomat or other government official; if you do not like the prospect, you do not go in for the career. Consequently, for 99 per cent of officials there is no problem. I do not mean this as a reflection on their characters. We have a decidedly good Diplomatic and home Civil Service, though I see no reason to go around trumpeting, as some people do, that it is 'the best in the world'. Who knows whether it is in fact better than the French, the Soviet, the American or the Chinese? The point is rather that government servants have to make up their minds to be not only efficient but also adaptable if they want to succeed.

Our diplomats would thus be well advised to keep a sharp eye on British domestic political trends; and also to keep on consistently close terms with journalists, both British and foreign. The hacks can on occasion tap disreputable but interesting sources of information more easily than the diplomat in his official position; and newspapers, radio and television have an ever-increasing impact on international affairs and on the style of diplomacy nowadays required to cope with them. The official diplomat, for his part, has some great advantages: elaborate cyphers and codes, some by now literally unbreakable; and the operations of the diplomats' private radio services, the Diplomatic Wireless Service. This decidedly important part of the diplomatic apparatus is, like others, permitted on a basis of reciprocity. The intrepid Queen's Messengers, or diplomatic couriers, also play a vital part, travelling all over the world by land, sea and air, sometimes with their diplomatic bags chained to their persons. They carry not only despatches and letters of every classified category, including the highest, but in the case of remote posts private letters too, which can do much to maintain the morale of their isolated recipients.

The truth is that diplomats are, in the nicest sense of course, licensed spies. (I shall have more to say later of the unlicensed variety.) US President Wilson naïvely insisted on 'open agreements openly arrived at'. But a moment's thought will show that except on the most non-controversial subjects this is out of the question. Open agreements reached by means of secret, or at least confidential, reporting and negotiation—that makes sense. In ordinary commercial business, after all, you often play your cards close to your chest if a big deal is at stake. In some critical confrontations statesmen will say that the moment for quiet diplomacy has come. But in a sense diplomacy should nearly always be quiet. To put it cynically, you can go so far as to start a war without any warning, or shouting and screaming, if you are so minded. Japan did so at Pearl Harbor. Occasionally there may be some point in losing your temper in a marked manner; but the diplomat must judge such occasions with care. Personally I would go further and say that on certain sensitive matters—involving, for instance, thermo-nuclear questions—secret agreements secretly arrived at may well be justified.

The diplomat's next important function is to represent his country in a true and effective fashion. This means that he must keep in touch with real life as it is lived in his own country, and the problems and attitudes of ordinary people in Britain and in the country where he may be serving. When abroad he will, naturally, have dealings mainly with people who hold power and can get things done—'the ruling few', as Sir David Kelly well called them. But it will not suffice for him merely to go the diplomatic and official rounds acting all the time as a diplomat and an official. When serving abroad he or she should nowadays establish contact with as wide a range of people as is practicable, and suitable, of the people of the host country. The aim is to establish an understanding, if possible a dialogue, between not only the governments but also the peoples of the two countries concerned. On crucial matters the diplomat abroad will follow closely the instructions he is sent from Whitehall, though not always uncritically or without putting forward his own suggestions. But in everyday dealings he should treat his foreign contacts as, in varying degrees, personal friends: showing readiness to help over their requirements; explaining patiently—and preferably pithily—why his own government's policies are not always as inconsiderate as they may seem; encouraging them to go to his country and see for themselves. Some originality in these matters, some going beyond the official brief, is to be encouraged; but the action taken and the discussions involved must be accurately reported to the head office. If the matters in hand involve delicacies which could adversely affect the diplomat's position *vis-à-vis* the government to which he is accredited, the time has come to turn to the Secret Service for advice and possible action.

On all these questions I have H.M. Diplomatic Service upper-most in my mind; but I believe that, broadly speaking, the principles apply universally.

Apart from service abroad, as many of our diplomats as possible should leave Whitehall altogether from time to time to work in, for instance, industry or journalism. In spite of their numbers and privileges, diplomats are increasingly concerned with ordinary, practical matters, particularly in the commercial and publicity spheres, and also with ordinary, practical people. A year or two every ten years, say, in business surroundings, dealing with business men and women, could be an effective 're-fresher'. This need is better recognized now than it was, but more could still be done.

THE QUESTION OF NEGOTIATIONS

A less important function of the professional diplomat today, formerly prized very highly, is that of conducting negotiations. The main reason is the speed of communications, which means both that the diplomat in the field can seek instant instructions from his head office and that the appropriate FCO minister can be on the spot, wherever it may be, in a trice to handle matters. (This is not always considered a blessing by the local ambassador.) Nevertheless, testing occasions do arrive. In Cyprus in 1959–60 we negotiated for eighteen months with the wily and meticulous Archbishop Makarios: Sir Hugh Foot as Governor, the commanders-in-chief of the Services, to whom I was attached, and myself on questions affecting the British bases. (Sometimes we felt we were negotiating with Sir Hugh Foot too.) True, Julian Amery came out as a Colonial Office minister 'for a few days' and stayed three months; but it was we who bore the brunt. Similarly in Berlin, we who were on the spot had to hold the line over the critical months in 1961–62 before and after the erection of the Wall. As described in the last chapter, Vice-President Lyndon B. Johnson and other politicians came out briefly and shored up the West Berliners' morale; but we had, day after day, to cope with outrages by the communist authorities which were not only maddening in themselves but often liable to escalate to a critically dangerous point if we on our side over-reacted.

The diplomat who is suitably equipped in these various ways should be able to grapple with the different categories of tasks. The emphasis in one job may be on strategic matters; in another economic; the next one may be preponderantly political or concerned with information; the next again with administration. The diplomat is not called upon to be an expert on each one of these, though special aptitudes will develop and duly be utilized. And, perhaps most important of all, his general training, and his feeling for policy based both on his instructions from higher authority and on his forward-looking capacity, will enable him to guide, and indeed manage, the experts in innumerable non-diplomatic matters who play an ever-increasing part in international relations.

THE INTERNATIONAL ORGANIZATIONS

One part of the diplomatic apparatus which is increasing in importance all the time, and will undoubtedly continue to do so, is that concerned with international organizations; and this is, on the whole, a hopeful sign. These bodies are indeed of such importance that I shall devote a separate chapter to them. Meanwhile it is appropriate to observe that they come in two categories: broad groupings devoted mainly to discussion, and alliances for defence. Examples of the former are the United Nations, the Organization for Economic Co-operation and Development in Paris, the Conference of the Committee on Disarmament in Geneva, the Council of Europe in Strasbourg. The alliances include the European Economic Community, the European Free Trade Association, the North Atlantic Treaty Organization, the Central Treaty Organization, the South-East Asia Treaty Organization, and on the communist side the Warsaw Pact Organization and the Committee for Mutual Economic Aid (CMEA or COMECON), the Common Market's opposite number. The question of British policy towards these organizations, and the apparatus we employ in playing our part in them, are of an importance that increases all the time. The first diplomatic action that every new nation takes is to send its diplomatic representative to the United Nations. There in the General Assembly, now over 130 strong (but without representatives of either West or East Germany, among others), the representative of, say, Barbados, Lesotho or Upper Volta can speak up with a vote equal to that of the USSR or the US. He may in due course be elected for two years as one of the ten non-permanent members to the Security Council of fifteen members. Burundi and Sierra Leone, for instance, are recent members, and their representatives take their turn as chairman. Much of the real power lies there, together with the veto which is wielded by the five permanent members of whom one, ridiculously, was until the other day Formosa.

Another move in the right direction is the increasing realization that diplomacy today is too important, and too complicated, to be left to the professional diplomats. It is not merely the fact that there are quite a few specialist attachés seconded from the home Civil Service to advise on such matters as science, aid, agriculture, culture, and so on. Our two top ambassadors, at Washington and Paris, are at present a banker and a politician respectively, both of them Privy Councillors and thus with direct access to the top policy-makers. This system works well, as it did with Lord Caradon until 1970 at the United Nations, and it could with advantage be extended to other crucial posts such as Moscow, Pretoria or Peking. Where an ordinary head of mission has to send back his reports through the regular channels, a man in Lord Caradon's position can at any moment pick up the telephone and get directly on to the Prime Minister. Again, the finishing touches to negotiations are often undertaken, and justifiably, by Ministers rather than by diplomats. But the tendency goes still further. With our constant dependence on foreign trade our businessmen get out and about more than ever in the world's highly competitive markets; and not only do they look to our embassies and the FCO for help and advice, they also reciprocate and often provide the diplomats with useful information and contacts. The same applies to journalists, authors, lecturers, artists and others concerned with foreign interests. The day of the diplomat who regarded all non-diplomats as lesser breeds without the law is totally past. Matters could indeed be improved by intensified cross-fertilization not only between the Diplomatic Service and industry but between various government departments. Full many a good diplomat may blush unseen in, say, the Ministry of Agriculture, Fisheries and Food, or the Home Office; and I have known some career diplomats who would have been better suited to the paperwork of domestic affairs in Whitehall.

THE DECISION-MAKERS

A basic and permanent feature of the British Diplomatic Service, and of many others, is of course the fact that policy is eventually made, and decisions and responsibility are taken, by people who are not diplomats at all, but are the elected representatives of the British people, plus the odd peer. It is right and proper that this should be so. One of Churchill's criticisms of Eden was that he was too much like a traditional diplomat. When he produced a beautifully balanced but indecisive paper with 'on the one hand' duly succeeded by 'on the other', Churchill commented that it contained every cliché except 'please adjust your dress before leaving'. The Marquess of Salisbury, when he was Foreign Secretary towards the end of the nineteenth century, was heard to remark mournfully about a similar document: 'Ah! how well I know those hands!' Naturally the interaction of politicians and diplomats is a constantly developing and changing process, depending not least on the characters, wills and capacities of those involved on both sides. Ernest Bevin, utterly untrained in diplomacy, made a good Foreign Secretary; yet, although he was a strong character, he depended more and more heavily on his officials. Selwyn Lloyd was a feeble Foreign Secretary who was content to play the part of his master's voice; this allowed Prime Minister Eden in 1956 to bully and deceive the Foreign Office into helping forward his disastrous Suez plans. Eden himself had been on the receiving end as Foreign Secretary under Neville Chamberlain before the second world war and under Churchill during it. Again, the officials of the FO were for many years sceptical about everything connected with the Common Market; it took Prime Minister Macmillan and other politicians to get matters moving, if abortively for a time. Michael Stewart spoke and thought like an official himself; consequently his officials had little difficulty in guiding him. George Brown was determined to get things done, and he did; not least the UN resolution of November 1967 on the Middle East, in favour of which the USSR withdrew their own resolution, and which still holds the field. Lord Chalfont, Minister of State at the FCO for almost six years from 1964, has complained that the career officials tended to try to bully ministers by presenting them with one-sided comments and proposals, admittedly elaborated with finesse, instead of giving objective descriptions of options and alternatives on which the minister could base his own decision.

One of the youngest top officials has commented to me that people like Brown and Chalfont made the mistake of thinking that diplomatic problems could, occasionally at least, be solved. He also condemned as a waste of time George Brown's liking for informal discussion, for batting problems back and forth with officials of no matter what rank. Here I would venture to disagree with the official. It is true that the nature of diplomacy is such that its practitioners should not go out for 'victories' in the military sense: first because these are seldom attainable in a world based on shifting sands; and secondly because a victory may seem like an humiliation to the other side, and so prove counterproductive in the longer run. (In passing, the same considerations apply to some military victories.) None the less, it is clear from the history of Europe since the last war, to mention only one sphere, that diplomatic problems often can, and must, be solved. Diplomats do not exist in order to play an eternal, unfinished, game of ping-pong. As to the question of informal discussions inside the Service, with junior officials also participating, this is much to be recommended on two counts: some of them are quite capable of throwing up fresh and good ideas, including the odd one that has been previously stamped on by a senior member of the hierarchy; and it is good for the junior official to be given this sort of opportunity of proving his mettle.

Lord (then Sir Harold) Caccia, when he was ambassador at Washington, said: 'If you are to stand up for your government, you must be able to stand up to your government', and in part that is true. Diplomats should not be entirely faceless. One of Sir Denis Greenhill's virtues is, or was until recently, that he is of an independent turn of mind. He was prepared to stand up to ministers and, what is more, when appropriate to speak like a minister himself.

The fact still remains that the diplomat's first duty is to collect information, then to collate it, and when appropriate to suggest action. There is something to be said for a measure of publicity for senior diplomats by way of lectures, writing for the press, appearing on television. A fairly recent head of the Foreign Office once remarked smugly that 'the Foreign Office does not advertise'. I think the FCO might in fact be better off if it did. But the essential basis must stay the same: in the last resort ministers must carry the responsibility for decisions. If a minister makes a fool of himself too often as a result of not heeding his officials' advice, he should go; but if, on the other hand, he makes an equal fool of himself by blindly following their advice, it is time to shift the officials concerned. And to take the functioning of the diplomatic apparatus a significant step further, ideally FCO ministers should have the strength of mind and ability to supervise and co-ordinate all Britain's official international relations even where other government departments are concerned. Clearly this cannot be done dictatorially or totally in every sphere. But the outstanding and vital example of this is the absolute necessity for FCO ministers, together with the Prime Minister, firmly to lay down the lines of our defence policy and commitments abroad, rather than allow defence ministers, plus their officials and officers, to hold the whiphand. This has not always been the case in the past—for instance when Duncan Sandys was Defence Minister and Selwyn Lloyd Foreign Secretary in 1957–59—and it needs watching in the future. It seems clear that in the United States today the balance has tipped the other way; and one of the lamentable results is the hamstringing of US diplomacy in many important directions.

THE END OF DIPLOMACY?

In making the point in the *Washington Post* that diplomacy has had its day, an eminent American commentator, Mr Zbigniew Brzezinski, goes on to assert that thanks to the revolution in communications, economics and weapons technology, foreign ministries and diplomats are now superfluous. But as he also proposes that the US embassy building in Grosvenor Square should be converted into a hostel for 'vacationing American students who can no longer unroll their sleeping-bags in Green Park' it can fairly be guessed that he is writing with his tongue in his cheek. More seriously, he contends that diplomacy has passed with the passing of the nation state, or in other words with the disappearance of rivalry for purely nationalistic reasons. But, desirable as that state of affairs would be, the fact of the matter is that we are nowhere near it as yet. In many ways the nationalistic rivalries are more tense and critical than ever before; and the need for shrewd and balanced diplomacy is that much the greater.

Mr Brzezinski finds a supporter in Anthony Wedgwood Benn. He declares roundly that 'foreign affairs' is a most absurd phrase, and that by the end of the first world war technology had caused foreign affairs to outgrow their old diplomatic definition. 'The idea that all the meaningful relations of any people with others who live in other countries can be squeezed through a network of narrow channels called foreign offices is at least a hundred years out of date.' He considers that the many world problems which exist must be tackled by a combination of technical, human and financial resources as well as by ideas and information. Both in multilateral and bilateral relations the field to be covered is almost unlimited. Diplomatic and political relations traditionally handled through the Foreign Office today form only 'a tiny sector' of the whole. Instead of boosting national interests all should rally to fight 'hunger, oppression and indignity'. Benn is sure that the younger generation understands these matters better than those in charge, and is more truly internationalist and anti-racialist. In place of unfruitful diplomacy we should aim to open up new areas of co-operation in the spheres of trade, technology, know-how, ideas. 'Later we might consider a world bonfire to burn all our national history books . . . and learn not to repeat the disastrous mistakes we have all made in the name of nationalism and patriotism.' I, as a member of the older generation, can only say that I wish Benn's ideas could be realized: I agree with them, as an ideal; but meanwhile we have a long and hard way to go through our epoch of proliferating nation states and groupings. For the foreseeable future we shall need diplomacy, though certainly of a new and developing type, to make sure that the world avoids a bonfire of a more catastrophic kind.

DR HENRY KISSINGER

I make no apology for referring again to this remarkable man, since he epitomizes more than anyone else today the style and thinking of the new diplomacy. He has defined diplomacy as 'the art of restraining the exercise of power'. Kissinger, like many politicians but few professional diplomats, enjoys power and its manipulation. He recognized early in his career at the White House that power lay with a strong President in Nixon, and not with a weak Secretary of State in William Rogers. Under Nixon's broad instructions he proceeded to establish with the foreign ambassadors in Washington, and not least with the Soviet ambassador, Dobrynin, the fact that it was he who counted in the big diplomatic game. Indeed, he was in touch with Dobrynin even before President Nixon's inauguration, and the relationship never looked back.

Metternich, one of Kissinger's heroes, believed that the key to success in diplomacy was 'freedom of action, not formal relationships'. Kissinger firmly believes the same; and his contempt for bureaucracy formed an immediate bond between him and Chou En-lai and, rather more surprisingly, Brezhnev. A close colleague of Chou En-lai said of Kissinger: 'There is a man who knows the language of both worlds—his and ours. He is the first American we have seen in this position. With him it should be possible to talk.' And it was. The spin-off, as Kissinger had planned, was that the Soviet leaders wanted to talk to him too.

Kissinger's achievements are obviously enormous.[1] Equally, they have put the noses of many career diplomats, in many countries, considerably out of joint.[2] There is only one Kissinger; what is clear is that the diplomats of the 1970s and 1980s have much to learn from a study of his methods.

SUMMARY

The nature of diplomacy is fundamentally, therefore, what it has always been: the management of international relations to the

[1] Historians will probably judge that President Nixon owes his second four-year term of office in no small measure to Kissinger's success in the new, highly flexible style of diplomacy.
[2] And others: his deputy, General Haig, was promoted some 140 places on the army list as a reward for his successful diplomacy.

mutual benefit of all concerned. The major limit to its effectiveness and capabilities stems from the fact that the decision on what
is the mutual benefit is taken by governments, and in most cases
unavoidably so. An outstanding example is the question of the
Vietnam war. By no means all United States diplomats, let alone
those of other countries, agreed that the involvement in, and the
escalation of, the war was to the mutual benefit of both the us
and South Vietnam. It has long been clear that those who dis-
agreed were right. But they were overruled by a succession of
us governments under pressure from the various non-diplomatic
groups and lobbies which I have mentioned. The professional
diplomats were then relegated to frustrating tasks such as running the embassy in Saigon, attending 'peace talks' with the
communist Vietnamese in Paris, chatting with the Chinese ambassador in Warsaw from time to time, and so on. This is an
extreme case; and even in this case the diplomats have no doubt
played a useful, defusing part on many occasions. Again, diplomacy depends on the economic, military, social, cultural, and
other resources of the nation or group concerned, as compared
with those of the other nations or groups with whom the diplomat is dealing. A representative of a small and poor nation
cannot expect to exert a major influence on the world's biggest
decisions. But skilful diplomacy can extract that important extra
benefit—and I repeat, benefit to all concerned in whatever the
problem at issue may be—which accrues from good management in this sphere, as in any other sphere of life.

As practised so far in the twentieth century the limitations of
diplomacy are all too clear. Diplomacy cannot prevent either
governments or other diplomats who have made up their minds
to use war as an extension of diplomacy from going ahead and
doing so: there has not been a single year in our century when a
major or a minor war was not in progress, or at the very least in
preparation. But there are plenty of examples of diplomacy avert-
ing war when the brink had been reached: Berlin and the Cuba
missiles crisis are recent cases in point. It can also mitigate the
effects of war up to a point while war is being waged; it can help
governments towards a peace settlement; it can play a part in
seeing that such a settlement is satisfactory, as it signally failed to
do at Potsdam. But it must be added that diplomacy has proved

unable at any stage to prevent the piling up of armaments. It has positively encouraged the setting up of dangerously rival alliances and blocs. Since the problems facing the world are now more ominous than ever, the question is: can a new style of diplomacy do better?

CHAPTER FOUR

Diplomacy and its Apparatus in the 1970s and beyond

THE STRUCTURE

It is easy enough to predict that economically the four super-powers will, barring accidents, be Japan, which before the turn of the century is likely to overtake the US in its gross national product; then the US; followed by the USSR and China. In passing, the Japanese performance will indeed be a miracle as their population is only a little over 100 million. The EEC has the potential to join this group, provided its members have the will to act in unity. If they have not, below these four will come the major powers, including undoubtedly West Germany, France, the UK, East Germany—another miracle, with a mere 17 million inhabitants—and Italy; and then possibly Canada, India, Brazil and others.

But the situation will be a good deal more complicated than this, for two major reasons: the relative strengths both of various economic groupings and of defence alliances, which of course depend heavily on the thermo-nuclear weapon. As regards the former, the trade exchanges between Japan and the US are statistically unbeatable, though Japan's trade with the rest of Asia comes within hailing distance. With the EEC expanding to nine nations, and getting on good business terms with EFTA, their economic force, including that of their associates in Africa and the Caribbean, should be not too far behind. The other great economic force is COMECON, led by the USSR and now strengthened by the addition of Yugoslavia and Cuba. Recent developments suggest that China will step up trade with both the US and the rest of Asia, thus becoming the fourth economic power. And we can fairly hope that these groupings will not merely compete with each other, thus gingering each other up, but also greatly expand trade between the groups and across ideological boundaries. It was good that in November 1971 an army of 108 American executives 'invaded' the USSR and saw Kosygin. 'You can hear the ice cracking,' commented their leader. This helped to produce a £52 million trade deal, representing an 85 per cent increase above the previous year's turnover.

Developments such as these will be fine for the inhabitants of the countries concerned, but a very serious caveat must be uttered: they will also increase the difference in standards of living between the developed and the developing countries to a literally dangerous extent, unless a way is found of greatly increasing not merely aid but trade with them.

NUCLEAR DEVELOPMENTS

As for thermo-nuclear developments, it is admirable that the Strategic Arms Limitation Talks have achieved, first, a slowing down of a very dangerous race. Next, we must hope for an agreement on a positive reduction in stockpiles. We shall need all the 1970s to achieve that; but the governments of the US and the USSR are capable of it. Also, there is no need to wait for that stage before NATO and the Warsaw Pact countries get together to discuss *détente* and serious measures of disarmament. They could do so without delay, any time; all the governments concerned have expressed their willingness, the British unfortunately with less conviction than the rest. The greatest help that the UK can give is to stay completely out of SALT and not give any interfering advice. Nor should we embark on any new ventures such as pooling our nuclear stockpile with the French. This would be futile; it would at the same time be provocative. Best of all, *pour encourager les autres*, we should allow our poor little so-called deterrent gently to phase out.

Very nearly as important as SALT is the question of securing wider adherence to the non-proliferation treaty. In spite of the first steps towards *détente* between China and the West, the danger must remain throughout the 1970s that China might cut loose and use a nuclear weapon, probably not against any of the present nuclear powers but for her own purposes somewhere in Asia. There is the further danger that the USSR might decide on nuclear castigation of China if the bitter quarrel between them gets worse; but my own view is that the Soviet government is too level-headed, and has studied the implications of such action so exhaustively that it is unlikely to do any such thing. The US and the USSR are not setting a good example in connection with disarmament. Not only do they 'play the numbers game' of mistrustfully and competitively increasing their nuclear stockpiles all the time; they have also positively increased the number of tests, underground of course, since the partial ban treaty of 1963. These run at about twenty a year each, and some, like Exercise Cannikin—Nixon's five-megaton extravaganza in the Aleutians —are deliberately as provocative as they can be. There is also the astonishing fact, publicly announced by a Defense Department spokesman, that the weapons systems now being built for that department will cost the US taxpayer $35,000 million more than was originally estimated. That increase is by itself nearly one and a half times Britain's total budget.

Another aspect of the danger is that many Japanese are bound increasingly to feel that as a super-power they are entitled to have nuclear weapons, if only to deter China from rash action. It seems short-sighted of the US government to encourage Japan to increase her non-nuclear defence capability; the day is likely to come before long when the new super-power is no longer content with American tutelage in the nuclear sphere. The probability is, therefore, that by the 1980s Japan will possess her own nuclear weapons; and however steady her governments may be this will constitute an added danger on the world scene.

Of the major powers neither West Germany, East Germany nor Italy possesses nuclear weapons. I do not foresee any great danger of their insisting on having them. The two Germanies are reliably covered by their faithful patrons; in this sense they cancel each other out and are spared, moreover, the hideous expense that nuclear equipment entails. Italy, too, is unlikely to commit the folly of going nuclear.

A great danger lies elsewhere: in the ranks of lesser powers, many of whom would be able to develop, buy, or acquire from some patron state nuclear weapons in the 1970s if they made up their minds to do so. Names often bandied about in this connection are Israel, India, Egypt and the Republic of South Africa. On balance, however, it is unlikely that the US and the USSR would permit a nuclear strike in the very critical conditions of the Middle East; and they will certainly continue to deploy their maximum intelligence efforts to detect the slightest signs of any preparations. On such a matter the CIA and the KGB would be ready to collaborate. India, one of the most irresponsibly governed countries in the world, is capable of making her own nuclear weapon, and since the cost, though large, could hardly affect the already wretched living conditions of the vast majority of her people, it is likely enough that she will do so in the next fifteen years. Indeed she would no doubt be happy to use it, presumably against Pakistan, in spite of the fearful punishment she would then receive from China; but here again India's new-found alignment with the USSR could well result in the latter exercising a moderating influence. Then Maoism, and other even more extreme forms of revolution for revolution's sake, are spreading in Africa, Latin America and Asia; and the widening gap between north and south in standards of living will provide exactly the conditions in which they will flourish more and more. In a word, I am pessimistic about the world's chances of escaping at the least a nuclear incident in the next twenty years; and in this connection, as in many others, Asia is the continent to watch in the 1970s.

There are several priorities for prevention. The existing nuclear powers must set a good example; more states must be cajoled into signing the non-proliferation treaty—and sticking to it; all those states whose main interest is peace—and over the years this will, unfortunately, by no means apply universally—must watch like hawks for every sign of potential proliferation; and when the incident occurs, as much level-headed influence as possible must be brought to bear, from all available sources, to limit its effects. All these are tasks for, and challenges to, diplomacy.

The British futurologist Robin Clarke, in *The Science of War and Peace*, is profoundly pessimistic. He reckons that, where 42·5 million people were killed in wars between 1900 and 1949, the probable figure for 1950–99 is 406 million, and for 2000–50 a terrifying 4,050 million, or more than the world's total population today. If it comes to that, diplomacy and pretty well everything else will have collapsed. What is certain is that wars and other upheavals will continue in Asia, Africa and Latin America; and that those of the super and major powers who have influence in any affected area must try to keep them within bounds. A detailed UN study points out that the international arms race absorbs two and a half times as much money as world expenditure on health, one and a half times as much as on education, and thirty times more than on economic aid. The chief culprits are, predictably, the US, the USSR, China, France, Britain and West Germany; but, very depressingly, the percentage increase in military expenditure is greatest in the developing countries. To put it bluntly and objectively, while 1,500 million people live in hunger and despair, and the ninety-six poor nations get no practical help from the third meeting of UNCTAD, the world now spends some £80,000 million a year on armaments. It is hardly surprising if from time to time a country like India decides to use her murderous toys.

The disarmament conference celebrated its tenth anniversary in Geneva with a confession that practically nothing had been achieved in all that time. An agreement was admittedly reached on destroying germ war weapons; but how will this be supervised in practice? Meanwhile President Nixon requests funds for a 600-ship navy. As for the current major wars, it will be a tremendous relief to the world when the US has withdrawn from Vietnam, as I believe she sincerely plans to do by 1973. Whether any real stability will be achieved in the Middle East before, say, 1975 seems doubtful.

CHINA AND THE FOURTH WORLD

When China at last took her seat at the UN in November 1971 she immediately and explicitly attacked the US, India and, by implication, the USSR. Her representative said: 'China belongs to the third world. The super-powers want to be superior to others and lord it over others. At no time will China be a super-power.' In practice, unfortunately for the world's peace of mind, that is exactly what she is, and she expressed openly her support of revolution everywhere. She immediately began a policy of wholeheartedly opposing any and every Soviet initiative; and even of refusing to take part in any multilateral discussions in which the USSR was involved, such as the disarmament talks and negotiations on the Middle East. The ugly little Indo-Pakistan war was of course, in its broader implications, a confrontation between the USSR and China; though it also brought the US and the USSR closer together over Asian problems. It will be hard work for diplomacy to effect a relaxation of this high tension in the 1970s. There is reason to fear the worst in this direction; and among other factors the US is faced with a very tricky balancing act.

It is helpful in analysing international prospects for the 1970s to recognize that we are accordingly likely to see the addition of a fourth world—the Maoist and extreme revolutionary—to the three that already exist: capitalist, Soviet communist and un-committed. The interests of the first two in maintaining peace and order, according to their different lights, coincide sufficiently for optimism to be permissible that diplomacy can bring them steadily nearer together, or, in a phrase which was much used a few years back, to indulge in competitive co-existence. From one angle the Middle Eastern situation, critical though it is, provides an example of this: for it could have been infinitely more dangerous if either the leading capitalist or the leading Soviet communist power had said the word to go full out.

An almost equally important objective of the diplomacy of the first two worlds in the coming years is to establish really sound relations with the third world, and to encourage a sound, that is to say peaceful, outlook on international relations there. This is going to be a very challenging and complicated business. It is relevant that Mao's Little Red Book has by now been distributed in more copies than the Bible. For the foreseeable future the fourth world will be in direct rivalry with the first and second throughout this sphere, and indeed beyond it.

The beginning of a *détente* between China and the US is a tremendously significant matter. But there is far to go and there are many corners to be turned before any close relations develop, and the existing profound and intensive rivalries on practically all international matters will continue unabated. Moreover, by the nature of probable developments in the twentieth and twenty-first centuries, if the point is ever reached where the four worlds have become one, or even two, some new world way out beyond Maoism may well have come into existence. Has not Miss Bernadette Devlin said publicly: 'I want Ireland to be a workers' state. I think that Russia and Mao's China are capitalist states. The ideal social state is yet to be founded.' If diplomacy could before the end of this century help to reduce the present four worlds to a reasonably balanced two, it would have done a magnificent job. Lord Trevelyan, who has served as head of mission in both China and the USSR, and described his experiences in his aptly named book *Worlds Apart*, is not unhopeful. Writing before the Kissinger era, he says: 'The Chinese were closer to the Americans than any other people. Perhaps, in spite of appearances, they still are. Who knows whether we shall not see in this century the ticker tape on Fifth Avenue streaming down on the head of a Chinese leader, and an American president standing on the Great Gate of Peking to receive the welcome of a thousand million Chinese?' A great step in this direction has already been taken. We have seen an American president greeted by thousands of Chinese; and standing on the Great Wall of China.

TECHNIQUES OF DIPLOMACY

These are, and will be, the macrocosmic aspects of diplomacy, with which only the top diplomats, ministers, and relatively few experts—for the most part non-diplomats—will intensively have to concern themselves. These questions will, or should, at the same time dominate and up to a point direct the activities of diplomats of all kinds, disciplines and grades, even though their personal contributions may be indirect and small. By this I mean that even, say, a junior British Council official in the wilds of Sri Lanka (Ceylon) should be on the look-out for bits and pieces of information which might just fill a gap in the jigsaw which depicts the political intentions of that country's government; while equally the defence attaché in an Arab country may well pick up a snippet pointing to a militarily based political revolution in a neighbouring state. The information officer at some embassy could well have a local industrialist friend who would be happy to throw light on economic trends and prospects; the labour attaché may be in a position to report on forthcoming developments in military procurement policy. Over the years I have found that one of the successful diplomat's principal quali-ties is the gift of getting people to talk to him, on no matter what subject. The traditional figure of 'the diplomat apart' has lost its utility for ever; but while we need and shall need specialists in every technical sphere to an ever-increasing extent, we shall also continue to need specialists in diplomacy, or the conduct of international relations, with the sharpest possible political judge-ment in view of the deep potential implications of such technical matters.

From my talks with top FCO administration officials I have derived an encouraging impression that the nature of diplomacy in the next decade or two is being seriously studied, and that attempts are being made to adapt the apparatus accordingly. To an increasing degree diplomacy will have to concern itself with everything from the sea-bed to outer space, and at least one deputy under-secretary (i.e. grade two official) with whom I spoke acknowledged this. One reason why there is a more forward-looking tendency is that the number of officials who began their careers before the war, and never did any other job, is now a mere handful; and it is a fact that among these only a few have managed to keep up with the times. The emphasis is now placed, rightly, on flexibility and good managerial qualities. The school-leaver entrant to the Service, and very few of these come from public schools, really can now hope to reach the upper grades of the Service. Conversely, a reform which I have advocated for some years is being put into practice: entrants are told fair and square that, as has for many years been the case in the Navy, they may be retired between the ages of forty or fifty, with decent compensation, if at those stages they appear less suitable than most to continue working. The sixtieth birthday is no longer a sacrosanct thing. Unfortunately there is still little prospect of anyone below the age of forty-six achieving the top three grades; this represents no progress on the situation fifteen or twenty years ago, when people like Sir William Hayter and Sir Patrick Reilly achieved just this. And this situation has the natural effect that fliers in their late thirties or forties are leaving the Service for more lucrative and responsible jobs, with at least equal interest of a different kind. If the Diplomatic Service wants to keep such people it will have to find a way to more flexibility in this connection. The intention is to have slenderized the Service appreciably by the mid-seventies. This is without doubt desirable; we shall see whether it is achieved. At the same time it is expected that the relative numbers in London will grow compared with those abroad. This too makes sense: a fair number of posts, and not least Washington, are too plushily staffed in view of the communications facilities now available.

One of the great attractions for an energetic diplomat in the coming years must surely be the chance of handling what is already a widely diversified list of problems, and can only become more so; always, of course, with full expert backing, since the diplomat himself cannot expect to have detailed knowledge or proper judgement on everything. A conspicuous example has been our negotiating team for the Common Market. At the head you have a politician, who by definition is an expert on nothing. At his elbow you have one of our ablest career diplomats, who can make suggestions on the technique of negotiation after he has himself been briefed by the experts on agriculture, fisheries, sugar, taxation and a wide range of other subjects, as well as by his junior diplomats. And this is only one example among very many of multilateral discussions and negotiations, as the long list of multilateral organizations shows. Some of the subjects quoted as departmental duties in the Diplomatic Service List are suggestive: telecommunications and stamp issues; meteorology; bananas, citrus, coffee, sugar, copra, phosphates; the monarchy in relation to the commonwealth; town twinning; the French Territory of the Afars and Issas; Tristan da Cunha; the Wilton Park Centre; vetting of manuscripts; reciprocal enforcement of maintenance orders; desalination; DAC, IBRD, IDA, IFC, CDC, CDFC, UNHCR, UNDP, UNCTAD, UNIDO. Believe it or not, this list of horrific initials is far from complete.

ABDUCTIONS AND HIJACKINGS

During the last three or four years diplomats have had to face some hazards of an entirely unprecedented order. I am thinking in particular of the abduction, followed sometimes by murder, of diplomats and other people considered valuable as hostages; and the hijacking of aircraft. These are all part of the fourth-world syndrome and the perpetrators, who in most cases are supporters of permanent revolution as a policy for international relations, are deliberately intent on disrupting the accepted system of law and order of any of the other three worlds. Diplomats are a particular temptation to them, both because they appear, though ordinary people, to mean so much to their countries of origin and of residence, and because they enjoy so many privileges which the revolutionaries—the 'urban guerrillas'— find irritating and obnoxious. I have little doubt, I regret to say, that these methods are with us to stay, and are likely to be intensified rather than the reverse. The FCO and the US State Department, as well as other foreign ministries, have no illusions about them; and of course the Tupamaros and their fellow gangs are well aware that they are on to a good thing. For many months we wondered what had become of Geoffrey Jackson, Her Majesty's Ambassador to Uruguay. All we knew for certain was that he was spirited away when driving in the centre of the capital, Montevideo, in broad daylight, in his official car, and with his security guard. He might be dead; he might be in the process of gentle—or not so gentle—brain-washing. We now know that he was under threat of death every day of his long captivity; and that his release was in no way due to the British or the Uruguayan government, but to Tupamaro machinations that led to the escape from prison of hundreds of their numbers, and hence of their relenting towards their victim. There has been no suggestion that the brutal action was aimed at him for personal reasons, or even that it was primarily anti-British. It was certainly intended to embarrass British–Uruguayan relations, and to make the local government look stupid. But above all it is a violent protest against the system as a whole, intended to show how brittle and even ridiculous it is; and we can be sure that many people, in many lands, welcomed the kidnapping.

What is the remedy? The FCO and the State Department are racking their brains, but it seems impossible to find a cast-iron solution. The FCO Chief Clerk spoke well and sensitively to a meeting of the Diplomatic Service Wives' Association on this problem. He told them that he had himself inspected all the most likely Latin American trouble-spots after Jackson had disappeared. He could give no guarantee of effective action against a repetition of the incident elsewhere, though security measures in general were being tightened up. Bitter though such occurrences were for the men involved, and their families, the British government felt obliged, for long-term reasons, not to give way to blackmail of this type. I agree with him, and so, I know, do many of our diplomats, including middle-aged men with families. Proper compensation would be given to the family for the suffering undergone, if the worst came to the worst. I can only suggest that, just as the Diplomatic Service inspectors keep up a constant round looking at our missions and consulates for general purposes, so a corps of really expert security inspectors—the FO has tended to be a bit amateur over security matters in the past—should keep up a continuous round. I would also suggest that the number of security guards should be considerably increased; and that they should be armed when on duty.

Do you remember the pictures of no less than three hijacked airliners, one British, lined up in the Jordan desert while the triumphant Palestinian guerrillas toyed with the idea of murdering all their occupants, eventually settling for destroying some millions of pounds' worth of aircraft? Governments protested to no avail. The British Embassy in Amman was impotent. To tell the truth, a thrill of excitement, and even of admiration, seized many people in Britain, and even more in some less advanced countries. The piratical achievement of course did the guerrillas' cause no good in the end, much less the Arab cause as a whole. But the cocking of a monumental snook clearly gave them great satisfaction for a while. There will be many more incidents like it. The statistics for the last three years are: 226 attempts or attacks, of which 153 in America, 19 in the Middle East, 54 elsewhere; 15 passengers dead and 39 injured; between 15,000 and 20,000 passengers and crew members affected. Up to the end of 1971 the proportion of successful hijacking was being reduced from the 1969 peak. But in 1972, up to July, this downward trend has been reversed.

These guerrilla operations were designed to disrupt normal relations between peoples and governments; and up to a point they succeeded. But the hijacking by the Libyan government of a British airliner containing two communist Sudanese leaders returning from London to take over their country, as they themselves mistakenly thought, has deeper implications. First, it is an outrageous act by a government with whom we are in full diplomatic relations; but it is no good going on as if international relations were stuck back in the epoch of courtly diplomacy. Clearly the brash young rulers of Libya reckoned that the risk of British displeasure was well worth taking for the sake of pleasing their friend President Nimeiry in the Sudan, whom the Soviet-backed communists had very briefly removed from power. There are other intriguing features. Why were the two communist officers in London while their coup was going on in the Sudan? Nimeiry's escape and return to power after only forty-eight hours was remarkable indeed; could the whole affair have been a put-up job by him and his *agents provocateurs* to enable him to clobber the communists, including one who was a minister in his own government? Who tipped off the Libyan government that the two officers were aboard that particular plane? What part did Libya's new friend Malta play? The case illustrates, among other things, to what a great extent rapidity and flexibility of thinking are required in international relations today and in the future. Presumably our Foreign Secretary knew when he begged Nimeiry not to execute the officers that not the slightest attention would be paid to his plea. And another important lesson must be learnt from the incident: since all the turmoil President Nimeiry has turned increasingly towards the Chinese communists.

Again, what is the remedy for hijacking? Apart from the X-ray inspection measures in force, which cannot be expected to detect all weapons and explosives, it seems to come in two parts. One is the installation of armed security officers aboard aircraft, which has had a good effect on us, Israeli and Ethiopian airlines. The other is a conference of all states with the object of agreeing to take sanctions against any state that shows leniency towards hijackers, for instance by blacking that state's aircraft and airports. With the four worlds all concerned there is no hope of full agreement on this topic, any more than there is on any other topic of international concern; but states who were likeminded in completely opposing hijacking could surely improve the present situation.

The Lod airport massacre of May 1972 epitomized all these

extreme fourth world characteristics. The attack was totally indiscriminate: the 100-odd victims belonged to half a dozen nationalities. It was carried out by Japanese on behalf of Palestinians. When the surviving Kami-kaze killer spoke in court he was in no way on the defensive: he expressly attacked all organized systems of life and promised more such incidents as the only way of bringing about world revolution. His sentence of life imprisonment, while obviously essential, will not deter other like-minded men and women. Only one Arab leader, the out-of-step King Hussein, condemned the outrage. According to CIA information, which seems likely to be correct, an international revolutionary terrorist organization central office was established in Zürich last year, with branch offices in Beirut, Tokyo and elsewhere. As a result, the activities of the Popular Front for the Liberation of Palestine, the Japanese Red Star Army, the Turkish People's Liberation Army, the Italian Red Brigade, the Uruguayan Tupamaros, the Irish Republican Army, and no doubt others, will be more efficiently and horrifically organized in the future. The relevance of all this to diplomacy is that in future happenings of this kind will proliferate, will have grave international repercussions, and must therefore be taken far more seriously into account than heretofore.

THE ANTI-DIPLOMATIC CORPS IN ALGERIA

The Libyan government's hijacking was outrageous enough; but far more so in a different way is the situation in Algeria. Here in Algiers you have what has been well called a mirror image of a diplomatic corps. The government welcomes representatives of liberation movements and terrorist organizations not only from Africa but from Asia and America too, and accords them quasi-diplomatic status. The effective ambassador of the US was until recently the Black Panther leader Eldridge Cleaver. He lived there in comfort and claimed to be developing a diplomatic service for the movement. Then, should a citizen of South Africa wish to visit Algeria he must apply for a visa to the Algiers office of the African National Congress, illegal in his own country. Mr Chiem of FUNK, the Cambodian revolutionary party, lives the ambassadorial life in some splendour. Altogether the Algerian government recognizes thirteen liberation groups, and it is fair to say that the British Embassy is about on a par with the representatives of El Fatah, the Vietcong, and the rest. This is the new diplomacy with a vengeance.

THE NEED FOR FLEXIBILITY

I have tried to show that the problems with which diplomacy will be called upon to cope in the 1970s and beyond include a great number, whether gigantic or comparatively tiny, of a totally new calibre; and the diversification will accelerate rather than slow down. I was glad to be assured by the FCO top management that the Duncan report was by no means accepted as the law and the scriptures, and specifically that its definition of the inner and outer circles of countries was already regarded as absurdly rigid. The idea, with which I was presented, of working on a sort of league table appeals to me as a good approach to the flexibility required in contemporary and forthcoming conditions. Arsenal, or say Washington, will never slip to the fourth league. But it could, given certain conditions, move down in the British diplomatic priority list several places, not only compared with other embassies but with some of our missions to multilateral bodies. Only a few years ago Libya was a sort of Peterborough, languishing in the third division; then oil came and King Idris went, and she is in division one or high up in two. There has been some surprise that our new ambassador to Moscow is merely a member of grade two; but without going into the merits of this particular case it is worth remarking that from 1953 to 1960 the incumbents were also grade two ambassadors, in the shapes of Hayter and Reilly. Broadly, the tendency should be to clip the staffs in our prestige embassies (and the consulates under their supervision) such as Washington, Paris, Rome, Madrid, Vienna, Brussels, The Hague, Lisbon, Stockholm and so on, for three reasons. First of all they happen to be too large anyway; these are missions run on what we used to call Rolls-Royce lines. Second, our bilateral relations with the countries concerned are of progressively smaller importance. And this is, thirdly, precisely because our representatives mingle with theirs in an increasingly important number of multilateral bodies, beginning with the UN, where all kinds of political, economic, defence and technical problems can be discussed, usually to better effect. In return for considerable cuts in the plush-embassy circuit, we can have a larger reserve of diplomats at the ready to move into those countries that thrust suddenly from league two to league one. By definition, these are apt to be countries with which we do not have so many contacts in multi-lateral bodies; and which present sudden, and often unexpected, threats to our interests.

An important facet of the new flexible diplomacy is the completely unofficial and personal activities of the volunteers for the Voluntary Service Overseas organization: girls who go to nurse in primitive conditions in Uganda or Malaysia, young men teaching in numerous developing countries, and so on. The equivalent US organization is on a vastly larger scale. Going a step further again, an intelligent young English man or woman who gets him or herself employed in an hotel or a garage in Switzerland, or who lives the ordinary life of a kibbutz in Israel, may well be rendering our diplomacy a service equal to that of a senior official diplomat. Flexibility is the key word.

THE UNITED STATES

It is hardly for a limey to speculate about the future of the US Foreign Service, but I will venture some ideas none the less, in general here and in more detail in chapter eight. The extreme malaise laid bare in the Macomber report of 1970, drawn up by US career diplomats themselves, is deep down part of the all-American malaise. How could a country which not only is, obviously, extremely powerful, but also in many ways truly great, have gone so wrong in its international relations and be so unhappy at home? This is not the place to analyse in detail the disastrous escalation of the Vietnam war, though it is worth noting that J. F. Kennedy and Robert McNamara should take a large part of the blame alongside Lyndon Johnson. The US government of Richard Nixon is at any rate beginning to understand that no one of the four worlds can set up to dominate the others; and great credit is due to him personally for stretching his neck out towards *détente* with the communist world, with the awareness that a large and powerful section of their respective nations would like nothing better than to see him fail. It is to be hoped that after the heart-searching of the Macomber report constructive steps will be taken to strengthen the efficiency and morale of the Foreign Service in the ways pinpointed by the report. It is tempting for a foreigner to say that a compact, highly professional Foreign Service is what is required. In practice, however, it is unlikely that the other foreign service, the CIA, will be downgraded; and although envious people of various nationalities may point to its failings and blunders, its achievements continue to be immense. Some might say that the system of having a second state department in the White House, with a staff of some 175 at the last count, harms the morale of the State Department itself and of the Foreign Service.

But what of the amazing Dr Kissinger, who only became an American in his teens, has never been a professional diplomat, and yet pulls off in his mid-forties the greatest coups in a most intricate field of secret diplomacy, Sino-American relations and the Vietnam peace? (His nearest Soviet counterpart is the curious Victor Louis, who has been officially allowed to visit Taiwan, Israel and Spain, and to peddle *Khrushchev Remembers* to the representatives in Scandinavia of US publishers. But the achievements are hardly comparable.) That part of the US diplomatic apparatus looks like staying and possibly becoming more, rather than less, influential. As for the custom of freely appointing generous party supporters as ambassadors, this is bound to be a continuing annoyance to able Foreign Service officers. But it would be a bold President indeed who abolished this long-established American tradition.

A recent comprehensive report by Secretary of State Rogers seems most sensible. It makes the points that harmony at home is paramount, that US foreign policy must help to achieve 'a new rational unity and purpose', and to overcome 'the deep and destructive divisions of the 1960s'. This 'new course' is to have various essential parts: greater sharing of defence responsibilities, implying a reduction of US forces in Europe and elsewhere; keener negotiation on issues like the Middle East and the arms race; the pooling of technological expertise in an effort to help the developing countries, among others. As regards Britain, it comes out strongly in favour of her entry into the Common Market, and states firmly that the US will not break the UN embargoes on the sale of arms to South Africa and on trade with Rhodesia. All these are excellent sentiments, and let us hope that they influence US diplomacy in practice. (Alas, it has already slipped up over trade with Rhodesia.) In return, the EEC countries must strengthen not only their ranks but also their unity of economic, political and defence purposes, if they are to stand up effectively and constructively to the other power blocs. We should work towards the day when there are no more ambassadors and embassies in western Europe; only the integrated representatives of the various nation-members of the united federation, or at least confederation.

THE USSR AND HER WORLD

The diplomacy of the USSR and her supporters will have to face a new balance of forces in the coming years, as will the rest of us. She is doing so already. Gone for ever is the old monolithic communist bloc. The old concept of the east European states as 'satellites' is totally out of date. Yugoslavia's bold surge to independence is being followed, quietly but effectively, by Romania. Poland is gently following a similar path. Czechoslovakia tried to move too blatantly, but 'liberalization' will come. East Germany, from being the greatest provocation to the West, is bidding fair to become a bridge connecting the two sides. Above all, the Soviet government has indicated in an unprecedentedly clear manner to the US that the old cold war is over.

She has good reasons to do so. The trend will continue, above all because of the vast new problems already presented by the emergence of China and the spreading of hostile Maoism— problems which will become greater as time goes on. If Western diplomacy is conducted skilfully enough, a steady *rapprochement* with the Soviet bloc should be possible, at the same time as a slower improvement in relations with China. At any rate the Soviet government will consider the former desirable, just because it considers the latter so undesirable. Our diplomats in the West should accordingly be instructed discreetly to increase their friendly contacts with the diplomats and other officials of the Soviet bloc, and this should in many cases be most easily and effectively achievable in the multinational bodies. But the balance must be delicately preserved or some catastrophic results could follow.

EAST GERMANY

One sphere in which the West has until very recently persisted in self-inflicting a wound, and in which the early 1970s are seeing a great easing, is that concerning the recognition of the German Democratic Republic. I am well aware that this subject is considered by many people to be my King Charles' head; but who would deny that *détente* in central Europe is of vital importance to the world? This well-established and orderly state has climbed from utter devastation at the end of the war to the ninth position in the world industrial league. With her mere seventeen million inhabitants she could overtake the UK industrially in the late seventies or the eighties. Willy Brandt's courageous Ostpolitik, for which he well deserves his Nobel peace prize, has enormously contributed to *détente* in central Europe. Thanks to his policy, in May 1972 the two Germanies signed their first ever bilateral treaty, about important transport matters. The preamble expressly states that this is an endeavour to develop normal, good-neighbourly relations between two independent states. It must in fairness be added that not far off half the West German people do not like Brandt's Ostpolitik. If the present opposition, the Christian Democratic Union, should win the next election, Europe could be back in the cold war; and our own present government would not be against this. Meanwhile, however, the Quadripartite Agreement of 3 June 1972 on Berlin has accorded *de facto*, though not, on the part of the Western allies, full diplomatic recognition to East Germany. And a few days later, still in June, far-reaching and fundamental discussions between the two Germanies began. I confidently predict that by 1973 they will both be members of the UN. A West German newspaper reported that the US authorities were beginning to plan for the establishment of an embassy in East Berlin; Britain is one of several nations now laying similar foundations. The recognition by the West of East Germany and of an independent West Berlin, under suitable safeguards, would be another enormous contribution to the less strained trend of the future. I happen to know that Brandt considers it would strengthen his hand, not the reverse, as so much of our press and so many of our conservative thinkers maintain. Then, long before the 1970s are out, NATO and the Warsaw Pact countries will be able to get down to serious discussion of a thorough-going *detente* with all the saving that would signify of enormous sums of money and the time and effort of hundreds of thousands of men in uniform on both sides.

THE ENERGY GAP

Many people in the United States, up to and including the President, are disturbed, and with justification, at the prospect of a fuel crisis there during the next ten to fifteen years, after which nuclear energy should step into the breach. With 6 per cent of the world's population, the US guzzles 33 per cent of the world's energy in the shape of coal, oil, gas and, on a small scale, nuclear products. It is doubtful whether the rate of increase of consumption can be safely met on existing lines from her resources and those elsewhere. This must influence the American diplomatic priority order. One good result could be that she is compelled to be more forthcoming to the OECD countries, and in particular to the Arab oil producers, with the result of a more balanced policy in the Middle East. Neither China nor the USSR faces a similar energy problem.

CHAPTER FIVE

Britain's Role

NUCLEAR MATTERS

The time has come to attempt to assess the priorities of a realistic
British diplomacy in the next fifteen years or so. The early 1970s
have thrown up a number of hopeful developments, and we must
do whatever we can to prevent them from turning sour. In some
contexts the best thing that Britain can do is stay out of the way,
not interfere, and speak only when spoken to. Thus the deeply
important Strategic Arms Limitation Talks can only be a dialogue between the super-powers. In the politically more confused
Middle East situation, again, the first glimmer of hope for a long
time—in the shape of the cease-fire—is entirely the result of bilateral super-power negotiations. The façade of 'four-power
talks' is a hollow one, and in fact tends to hinder progress. The
USSR can only be annoyed by the unwarranted pretensions in the
context of the Middle East of the two ex-colonial powers,
Britain and France, whom they regard with some justification as
normally ganging up with the US in a sort of Western front. If
and when asked for support or advice by the US we should give
it, that is all. This applies right across the board. It is an excellent
thing that there is a hot-line between Washington and Moscow.
It is a good thing that there is rapid direct communication between the White House and Downing Street. But it would be
silly to pretend that they are on a par. If you set up more than
one hot-line you debase the currency; all the lines become tepid.

To revert to specific developments: in Vietnam the signs are
vastly more hopeful as the peace agreement begins to take effect.
Britain has no say in this matter. As regards Willy Brandt's
admirable initiatives designed to ease relations with the USSR,
Poland and East Germany, we should give him every possible
backing. If all goes well this should lead to a European security

conference, long advocated by the communist states, at which it would be appropriate and convenient for NATO to discuss with the Warsaw Pact countries the reduction of the forces facing each other in central Europe as a further step towards a general easing of tension. This will be all the easier as the US government will certainly wish to reduce its forces in Europe before long.

In this context, as in that of the highly significant nuclear non-proliferation treaty which is collecting signatures at a good pace, Britain can and must make an important contribution in the 1970s. First she must phase out her nuclear weapons, that is, the Polaris submarines. The truth is that if the British homeland is involved in another war it cannot be defended. The idea of deterrence is often used very vaguely. Who is deterred by our two Polaris submarines wandering about the oceans? Obviously not the USSR. Nor, for that matter, the anti-British elements in Anguilla or Ulster. Indeed, even the nuclear might of the US does not prevent the Vietcong from fighting on against her. West Germany? She has for some time been a good ally of ours, and the possibility of a military clash in the next fifteen years seems most remote. A subterfuge such as uniting our nuclear weapons with the French—an unlikely accomplishment anyway—would be futile. Any idea of a joint NATO nuclear weapons system, including of course the West Germans, would put us straight back into the cold war. We must resist every temptation to ask the US for more modern nuclear hardware; in a moment of generous aberration, or as part of some cumbersome package, they might even agree. By renouncing our minimal nuclear power we can save a lot of money and devote it to more worthwhile projects; and set a good example in the field of non-proliferation and disarmament generally. It seems likely enough, unfortunately, that a limited nuclear war, probably involving China, may occur somewhere in the seventies or eighties. But that unpleasant problem can only be dealt with by the US or the USSR, or both together. It is beyond the capacity of Britain or France. The only direction in the nuclear weapons sphere in which we might be usefully employed is in collecting intelligence on developments by potential enemies and passing it on to the US. But it seems unlikely that we are as well equipped to do this as they are; and in any case this comes under the heading of espionage rather than diplomacy.

In general Britain should help her economy by reducing her armed forces strictly to those required for political purposes; this boils down to NATO and to the occasional context in which we might be asked to help in what we consider a good and practicable cause. In my opinion this does not include Ulster, which in any case will sooner or later, and almost certainly by, say, 1985, be reunited with her mother Eire. Nor does it include south-east Asia, where Malaysia and even the US have tried to make us stay on but will in the upshot get on perfectly well without our forces, except on the reasonable scale recently agreed under ANZUK. It most definitely does not include the Persian Gulf, where we have sensibly taken action on the decision by the Labour government to withdraw. If our nominal collaboration in SEATO and CENTO, together with annual contributions of a mere £81,000 and £60,000 respectively, bring comfort to our friends in those parts, there can be no objection to that. All other prestige considerations should be forgotten. We shall in every way be better off without them. This is quite different from becoming another Sweden: we are deeply involved in the NATO alliance, we intend to be deeply involved in the EEC one, and our commerce and diplomacy can still wield a world-wide influence if properly directed.

COMMERCE AND THE EEC

So much, temporarily at least, for nuclear diplomacy, intertwining as it does with the economic and commercial factors which are also basic to Britain's position in the world. We have to do two things, which are simple to describe but difficult to realize in practice. With our static population and relatively weak financial situation we have to increase productivity and production at two or three times the present rate in order to keep up with the other nations in our league. Secondly, we have to sell ourselves and our products wherever we can. To a limited extent skilful diplomacy and publicity can make up for a lack of swelling production. Here I have no doubt that we have been right to go bald-headed for membership of the Common Market. It has helped immensely to bring prosperity to its members; in the longer run it would do as much for us, if we can prove ourselves adaptable enough to be a worthy member of it. By 1980 it could be a great new world force, with Britain as one of its leaders. As we know, the US would warmly welcome this; and it could pave the way towards a comprehensive *détente* with the European communist countries and have a steadying influence in almost all parts of the world. What is the alternative for Britain? Not EFTA, helpful though it is, because it by no means has the potential of the EEC and because it should become part of it, and thus strengthen it, anyway. Should Britain become submerged in a North Atlantic-cum-Australasian commercial combination? Certainly not, for all sorts of reasons. Her identity might well be swamped; and this rich white man's league would not only incur odium in three-quarters of the world but would jeopardize the future of Europe too. Should Britain, alternatively, become a Sweden? It would be a great waste of our capabilities.

THE COMMONWEALTH

Finally, should Britain concentrate more on the Commonwealth? Forget it. The Commonwealth as such is a diminishing economic and political asset. It dwindles year by year. We would do well to slough off some of our financial and commercial responsibilities in that direction; a start has already been made. Canada, Australia and New Zealand are firmly in the US sphere of influence, and are more prosperous than Britain. India is in such complete turmoil that perhaps she is the one country in the world which might profit from a dose of communism. At the same time we should put great effort into not just maintaining but increasing our commercial exchanges with those Black African countries—whether members of the Commonwealth or not—where we have a good, often predominant, trading position. This is a valuable asset in our bargaining situation *vis-à-vis* the EEC; and the prospects are rich and expansive. Indeed they are far more so in the longer term than our trading prospects with the South African and Rhodesian Republics. Happily, therefore, self-interest here coincides with our duties, as members of the human race and of the United Nations, to strengthen the millions who oppose apartheid. As for the reason given in favour of supplying armaments to the Republic of South Africa, to the effect that the

Soviet navy is threatening the 'sea-lanes' in that part of the world, this has a hollow ring. In the first place the proposal is directly contrary to a UN resolution, more than once confirmed. Secondly, the nineteenth-century concept of 'sea-lanes' no longer applies in the strategic conditions of the late twentieth century, where new forms of power—nuclear, submarine, air, as well as those of the surface navy—make such a concept ridiculously limited. Finally, the fact that the Soviet navy is roaming the high seas in the same way as the US navy in no way implies that, for the foreseeable future, she will be committing aggression against the merchant navies or fleets of other countries.

THE UNITED NATIONS

For the first time since the United Nations was formed, in the years 1964–70 Britain treated it seriously, largely thanks to our head of mission there, Lord Caradon. In other words, instead of complaining, like Douglas-Home, about the 'double standards' observed there, as if it had been set up for the exclusive purpose of furthering British interests, we used it as a valuable meeting ground of practically all the nations in the world, and did our best to support its dignity and effectiveness. Many fruitful contacts have been established there with the developing nations. The Brown–Caradon resolution of November 1967 about a settlement of the Arab–Israeli imbroglio was something of a triumph, since it superseded one by the USSR which they voluntarily withdrew.

It is most important that we should patiently continue on the same path. Of course there are double standards in some ways, just as there are widely differing standards of living between the richer and the poorer nations. The UN is useful in that it gives us the continuing opportunity to learn about those differences and to work as far as possible against their increasing. It does us real harm in the world to oppose a resolution in the General Assembly demanding that there should be no independence before majority rule in Rhodesia, as we did in November 1971; and to be defeated by 102 votes to 2, those of Portugal and South Africa. Again, although we have so far kept this issue out of the United Nations, our obstinate and unsuccessful policy in Ulster earns us world-wide opprobrium, not least in the US, and gives a most acceptable handle to 'anti-imperialist' propaganda in the communist countries and beyond. In the sphere of aid to developing countries, there is much that we can learn in the UN and its various agencies, such as UNCTAD, dealing with the question of how to offer aid in both the most tactful and the most practical manner. Let us hope that before long Britain's official contribution in this direction will attain the not over-munificent proportion of 1 per cent of her GNP.[1]

Nobody pretends that the UN is perfect or always effective; it can only become, say, 50 per cent more effective when the superpowers have come closer together. But we should work wholeheartedly towards helping to improve it. Secretary-General U Thant described the situation and the tasks for the future in a very frank speech in Geneva in July 1970, opening the 25th annual session of the UN's Economic and Social Council. The purpose was to approve plans for the second 'development decade'; but was it much use, he asked, making such plans 'if they are likely to be rejected outright for outdated military and political reasons. . . . The people are becoming impatient. New tensions are mounting. How much longer can we continue on the present path of division, suspicion and waste, in a world already united by scientific and technological progress?' The UN had been a useful channel for diplomatic communications, and had exposed to the world cases of the use of force, territorial ambitions, and other 'national misdeeds'. But, on the debit side, the UN had failed 'to curb the armaments schizophrenia' or to pacify the Middle East and south-east Asia. How was it universal as long as it did not include China, or the divided countries of Germany, Vietnam and Korea?

And, as the 25th General Assembly met in mid-September 1970, U Thant uttered another grim warning: he reckoned that the UN had at the most ten years to come good, or it will fade away. Seasoned observers in New York were not optimistic about this session. A few things are for sure. Fiji and Bahrain were admitted and swelled the membership to 128; since then it has increased to over 130. Many of the world's leaders appeared and spoke; some good may come of their private contacts but little from their public pronouncements. Among the 108 items

[1] It is at present approximately 0·75 per cent.

on the session's agenda were plenty deploring 'the situation' in the Middle East, in South Africa, in Vietnam, as regards nuclear disarmament, and so on; they will lead to little effective action. President Nixon chose this moment to publish the report of a US commission on the UN, headed by the former US ambassador to the organization, Henry Cabot Lodge. It concludes that the UN has two main defects: 'the failure of its members to make it the paramount means for maintaining international peace and security; and its misuse as both an unwieldy and ineffective debating society and propaganda platform'. In particular, its 'inability to act when the super-powers clash has produced a dramatic drop in public support for the UN in the US'. These are factual criticisms; equally factually, it is for the super-powers to give a lead and to make something effective of the UN, instead of wasting their energies on highly dangerous bickering.

As a postscript to these gloomy prognostications I must add that unfortunately the UN's session proved them all too true. Since then one sound, if overdue, action has been taken, thanks to agreement for once between the US, the USSR and China: the People's Republic has taken its rightful place on the Security Council. But otherwise the UN's effectiveness and credibility have, sadly, waned rather than waxed.

All in all, then, here is an ambitious programme, a terrific challenge, for the British diplomatic apparatus, among others, in the 1970s. Our new diplomats, and specialists from various quarters inside and outside the government service, should play an active part in the numerous multilateral bodies of which Britain is a member, whether they are agencies of the UN or not. As for 'normal' bilateral relations with our old friends such as the US, of course we want to keep them as cordial as can be. Here it must be remembered that in today's rapidly developing and shrinking world fewer and fewer questions can be handled strictly bilaterally; and that it is always better to look forward rather than back. This applies even more strongly to our relations with the communist countries, where there is indeed ample room for improvement and, at last, some prospect of bringing it about. So there is every likelihood of the 1970s being an exciting epoch for diplomacy, and even a highly constructive one provided that the international organizations, and the member nations, can find the right types of diplomat and the appropriate diplomatic apparatus.

Since Dr Kissinger looms so large on the contemporary diplomatic scene, I would add that I see no likelihood of a counterpart in the British system of conducting affairs. Indeed, I see no need for one as Britain becomes progressively more integrated politically into the Community. Our closest equivalent is Lord Goodman; though he carries more weight in one sense, he could never come near to doing so in the diplomatic sphere.

SUMMARY

Britain's first diplomatic objective in the 1970s must therefore be to make herself a worthy and ever more fully integrated member of the European Communities, and to help the alliance, as smoothly and as rapidly as possible, towards political unity. With this new-found strength she can also help to lead in the direction of *détente* between western and eastern Europe. She must retain in NATO the minimum force necessary to serve this same political purpose: the defence aspect is in most ways illusory. Next, western Europe will maintain close ties with the US, on a better basis than at present as its united strength increases. Britain should, without illusions, be active in the UN and the more practical of its dependent bodies. We should study far more seriously the practical ways of stepping up trade and aid in the direction of the developing countries. It will be useful to maintain our Commonwealth ties, in so far as the other members wish it. We must face up to shedding responsibility for Ulster and Rhodesia. These, broadly, are our diplomatic priorities for the 1970s.

CHAPTER SIX

Her Majesty's Diplomatic Service, and the Foreign and Commonwealth Office

In order to get a clear picture of the British diplomatic apparatus today and of its future prospects, it is necessary to delve slightly into the past. In the last twenty-five years four governmental reports have affected the apparatus to a greater or lesser degree. For the moment we can call them by the names of their chief instigators: the Eden report of 1943 which Bevin put into force in 1946; the Plowden report of 1964; the Fulton report of 1968; and the Duncan report of 1969. Very broadly, the main aim of them all was the modernization and democratization of the Service; the Fulton report concerned itself with the home Civil Service but has had some considerable effect on the Diplomatic Service too.

THE EDEN WHITE PAPER

The White Paper of January 1943 was short and had a sweeping title: *Proposals for the Reform of the Foreign Service.* The new, American-style appellation of the Diplomatic Service was one of the reforms; it lasted less than twenty years, after which the traditional name was revived. The Foreign Service was intended to amalgamate five independent components: the Foreign Office, the Diplomatic Service, the Consular (the members of the first three of these were interchangeable already), the Commercial Diplomatic, and the Information Services. This was clearly a sensible intention. But it was not as sweeping as it appeared. In practice, of course, the Foreign Office and the Diplomatic Service had always been regarded as the plums, and some bright members of the other services had managed to cross into them. Even after the reforms, the same two branches continued to be so regarded, as they are to this day. Transfers into them were made

somewhat easier, that was all. Similarly, the Service was divided
into four branches, A to D, with improved chances of elevation
from a lower to a higher branch. In practice, however, this frequently had the result, particularly in posts abroad, of causing
social friction between the branches and piling up chips on
shoulders when promotion did not come. Another move in the
right direction made it easier for people with no private means to
get along in the Service; but here again it is only in the very few
last years that allowances for education, holiday flights between
boarding school in Britain and posts abroad, rent in Britain, and
suchlike have been adequately and imaginatively developed. In
sum, the Eden–Bevin reforms were an honest attempt to meet
the criticism that our senior diplomats came from too narrow
and unrepresentative a social class, and that the Service was over-
rigidly stratified. The fact that it was Bevin who put them into
force shows that the Labour government appreciated their progressive intention. In practice, however, the impetus flagged
over the years after the war, as in so many sectors of British life.
People from sources other than public school and Oxbridge did
not flock to join branch A of the Foreign Service. And inside the
Service destratification did not exactly proceed apace.

THE PLOWDEN REPORT

After the nine pages of the Eden White Paper came the massive
180-odd of *Miscellaneous No. 5 (1964). Report of the Committee on
Representational Service Overseas appointed by the Prime Minister
under the Chairmanship of Lord Plowden. 1962–63*. The seven
members of the committee were, of course, to a man members of
the inner Establishment; and though a few bodies and individuals from outside Whitehall were consulted, the emphasis
was heavily on the views of officials. The committee was not
asked to look at the structure of the Foreign Office as such.

Many of the committee's fifty-two 'principal conclusions' were
sound, though it seems surprising that some of them came so
late in the day. For years foreigners had been bewildered by the
multiplicity of our departments and services dealing with overseas affairs, and a partial improvement was now proposed: a
unified Service including members of the Foreign Service, Commonwealth Service and Trade Commission Service. Incredibly,

the three London departments—the Foreign Office, Commonwealth Relations Office and Colonial Office—were still to remain separate. Greatly daring: 'This unified Service might be known as "H.B.M. Diplomatic Service".' This in fact came about on 1 January 1965. Time passed until the Colonial Office merged with the CRO to form the Commonwealth Office on 1 August 1966. Not until 17 October 1968 was the interdepartmental feuding settled, and the combined Foreign and Commonwealth Office born.

Other useful proposals of the Plowden report were those for a new grade structure which formed the basis of the one existing today; the encouragement of secondments between the Diplomatic Service and government departments at home; and a call for greater specialization in languages, which had been somewhat neglected before. Emphasis was also laid on the importance of a unified communications centre, completely lacking till then; and economic and commercial work were for the first time to 'be regarded as a first charge on the resources of the Diplomatic Service'. The Committee reported that 70 per cent of successful entrants into the senior branch of the Foreign Service came from public schools, and no less than 94 per cent from Oxbridge. It expressed the opinion that it was important to break this monopoly; but no very practical steps were suggested. Both language and mid-career training were said to be important: but 'a Diplomatic Service Staff College is not practicable at present'. One or two ideas were particularly forward-looking: the volume and direction of work should be carefully assessed each year; 'policy planning' should be considerably developed, with the help of outside experts; there must be a new and improved system of allowances, particularly in connection with family responsibilities. The great importance of suitable office accommodation, by no means least in London, was stressed, though matters are if anything worse in this respect today.

A few points were handled less satisfactorily. A note at the beginning of the report pointed out that certain matters were omitted 'on security and similar grounds', and gave the assurance that they were of small significance. 'Similar grounds' is vague and broad; and even if the assurance satisfied some readers, others will regret that there is no reference to the activities of MI6 or MI5, as they were then called, both of them vital to the diplomatic apparatus. Then the report is rather leary of 'functional departments', and considers that technical assistance overseas should be 'an integral part of the tasks of the Diplomatic Service', whereas it surely calls for trained experts and an independent approach. Similarly, the report has little to say about the numerous international bodies which play such a vital part in diplomacy today, and of the special type of diplomacy required from our representatives on them. Finally, though nine government departments were consulted, the Ministry of Defence was not among them: a serious lacuna because of the importance both of defence matters in our broad diplomatic strategy, and of getting such matters in their right place, which is strictly subordinate to our diplomatic requirements and capabilities.

As soon as the Labour government came to office in 1964 it pressed ahead with reforms on the lines of the Plowden report, as it had with the Eden proposal some twenty years earlier, culminating in the setting up of the combined FCO in October 1968. By then the Fulton Committee on the home Civil Service had reported; and the Duncan Committee had started work.

THE FULTON COMMITTEE REPORT

The Fulton Committee report of 1968 impinged on the diplomatic apparatus in three main ways. First, it advocated greater flexibility as regards movement not only from department to department within the government service but also between that service and industry, business, journalism and the academic world. Later on, the Duncan Committee was to approve this idea specifically with reference to the Diplomatic Service. Second, Fulton came out strongly in favour of further democratization by recommending the abolition of the distinction between the administrative and executive classes and, further, the opening up of far more tempting career possibilities to the clerical grade. Duncan gave some support, not over-warm, to these ideas; but the FCO, I am glad to say, has gone some way towards putting them into effect. To take a small but practical example, the two forms of grade five, administrative and executive, have now been merged.

Perhaps most important of all, Fulton called for greater specialization and professionalism. On this the Duncan Committee was to drag its feet, with a good deal of shuffling around the question of 'professional generalists' being more desirable than 'generalist amateurs'. But who in this day and age can afford any type of 'amateur' in its diplomatic apparatus? This was a regrettable lapse on the part of the Duncan Committee. It is only fair to add that an under-secretary in the Department of Employment has publicly and at length propounded the view that after Fulton came only 'the pseudo-revolution'; that the coalescence from 1 January 1971 of the administrative, executive and clerical classes in the home Civil Service was an illusion; and that the Whitehall mandarins continue unhampered on their omnipotent ways, wholly free from public scrutiny and easily dealing with any attempts at intervention by their ephemeral ministers.

THE DUNCAN COMMITTEE REPORT

It might seem that this Committee—'The Review Committee on Overseas Representation'—came rather hard on the heels of Plowden. But it was summoned by a different government; its members formed a different kind of team; and its terms of reference were far more lengthy and specific. Foreign Secretary Michael Stewart invited three men in August 1968 'to aim to report within six months' on various knotty problems. They missed that target, but turned in a report of over two hundred pages by June 1969. They were Sir Val Duncan, a dynamic leading industrialist; Sir Frank Roberts, whose sparkling diplomatic career had just finished with the embassy at Bonn; and Andrew Shonfield, a distinguished writer on economic and international affairs. They were asked 'to review urgently the functions and scale of the British representational effort overseas (including defence and other attachés and advisers . . .) in the light of the decisions on foreign and defence policy announced by the Government on 16 January 1968, the balance of payments, and the changing international role which these imply for the UK, to make recommendations particularly on the furtherance of British commercial and economic interests overseas and . . . to consider the value . . . of information submitted by overseas posts in the political field; to have regard to the functions and scale of representation by other major western European countries; to bear in mind, in the light of the current need for the strictest economy, the importance of obtaining the maximum value for all British government expenditure and the consequent desirability of providing British overseas representation at lesser cost; and to aim to report within six months in order that the benefit of any savings may accrue as soon as possible.' A mouthful, but terms which pinpointed several vital issues and went a good deal further forward than those given to Plowden. In effect, they called for an urgent review of our diplomatic apparatus abroad in the post-devaluation period, with a view to matching the government's deliberate world-wide reduction of defence commitments; to boosting our commercial capability; and to effecting economies in connection with the apparatus. Once again, this Committee was not asked to look at the Foreign and Commonwealth Office as such.

The report plunges right in with the statement that for the purposes of designing a system of representation for the mid-1970s two broad categories of countries should be sharply distinguished: the advanced industrial countries, where British representation will have far-reaching responsibilities; and the rest of the world, including the Soviet bloc and the under-developed countries. Our missions would be divided into 'comprehensive' in the 'area of concentration' which covers all Europe, China, and certain important countries in the 'outer area'; and 'selective missions' in the rest. The latter would do very little political reporting and have a minimum strength of only three UK-based officers each. As a result economies of staff and money would be effected. Further economies could be effected, without loss of efficiency, by sending in diplomats from other posts on periodic visits. This method has in fact been employed for some time, though the experiment of John Wilson commuting between the FCO and Chad, as head of the Central African department in the former and ambassador to the latter, is original, and none the worse for that. This broad division might prove administratively convenient, but it could have been more tactfully expressed in a public document; for to many underdeveloped countries it must imply a ganging-up of the richer countries to ensure that the economic gap between them and the rest, already wide, keeps on widening. Andrew Shonfield, indeed, wrote soon after that the distinction was too rigid. However, the report went on to stress the need for adaptability by diplomats to rapidly changing circumstances, and greater flexibility as regards promotion, and movement both to and from the Service as well as inside it, by merging the administrative and executive classes. It recommended increased modernization and mechanization of the Service's procedures. In particular, while the team found much evidence of progress in the management of the Diplomatic Service today, it considered that in certain respects, such as accounting practice, there was positively over-administration, with no additional efficiency. 'At one mission we visited it was estimated that the introduction of mechanized accounting at a capital cost of about £1,500 would save £2,000 a year in local staff wages.' In a different sphere it called for 'new high-level machinery to ensure adequate strategic thinking on organizational questions as they affect the formulation of policy'. This in effect meant a body of senior officials from both the policy-making and the administrative sides who would legislate on the future shape of the Service in such a way as to keep its organization as well adapted as possible to its probable tasks and responsibilities. You might call it a think-tank of high-grade official futurologists.

The report made two sound points when it stated that economic and commercial work was the most urgent task and 'a large part of the substance of political work'; and particularly in connection with what it called the 'new diplomacy', which involves increasing contacts between specialists of numerous kinds in multilateral bodies, and for which type of diplomacy our officials must increasingly be trained. Diplomats should stay longer at each post abroad and, once more, should serve to a greater extent in industry and at the Board of Trade. Rapid communications, such as telex, should be more frequently used, and computerization at the centre could help a great deal. Our information services—the word propaganda is still taboo in connection with our diplomacy—should deal mainly with commercial matters, and not try to put across Britain as a super-power. The staffs employed abroad on information work could probably be cut by

50 per cent. The committee thought that the BBC and the British Council were doing good work, though the latter's staffs should be more familiar with science and technology. A recommendation that the balance of the British Council's activities should be shifted towards western Europe seems to me misconceived: it is precisely in remote and underdeveloped countries that the Council can effectively provide services which are otherwise difficult to come by.

The report further recommended that consulates, too, should concentrate on commercial work, and traditional consular services should only be provided by certain larger posts. To reduce the cost of passport work, passports should have 'limp covers' so that they could be mechanically processed; this drew from Sir Alec Douglas-Home as Foreign Secretary the comment: 'Over my dead body'.

On civilian and service attachés the Committee proposed considerable reductions in numbers, though some scientific, financial and defence experts would continue to be needed. As in earlier reports, nothing about the expert intelligence and security bodies was allowed to appear. Finally, the report stated that something needed to be done urgently to provide modern and well-equipped offices in the right locations at posts abroad; far too many were still rented so that considerable expenditure in foreign currency was being wasted. At home the centralization of staff in one modern building, in place of the seventeen heterogeneous buildings at present occupied, would greatly increase efficiency and lead to substantial savings of staff and money.

Obviously some of the Committee's recommendations would lead to increased expenditure in the short run; that is life. But on the credit side, in the longer run the report lists the reduction of the information staff by half, and of political reporting outside the 'area of concentration' by a substantial amount; administrative simplifications; modifications in traditional consular services; the restructuring of the civilian and defence attaché system; the improvement of accommodation abroad and at home. They forecast that these changes could be complete by the mid-1970s, bringing a saving of total expenditure between 5 and 10 per cent. If realized, that would be a considerable achievement. A somewhat smug comment to me by a very senior official was that all the best ideas in the report had originated in the FCO itself.

The report was published on 16 July 1969, and three days later Michael Stewart made a typical statement in the House of Commons. While warmly welcoming the Committee's general approach he said that before the government could give specific endorsement to the conclusions it would need to go further into their probable consequences, their implications for the standard and range of Britain's services overseas, and their effect on British foreign policy as a whole. I shall have further comments later on the report's impact.

NUMBERS AND STRUCTURE OF THE DIPLOMATIC SERVICE

The annual official Diplomatic Service List, which first appeared in its present form in 1966, states blandly that the Service has some 6,000 members. This is, however, by no means the whole story as it refers only to relatively senior and established staff. A more accurate figure would be about 10,000; and even this is not complete, for there are in addition some 9,000 staff locally engaged abroad by the Diplomatic Service.

Practically all members of the Service are expected to serve both at home and abroad, though career patterns naturally vary according to the different aptitudes of different officials. The Service, like all other branches of the Civil Service, is heavily stratified: not only are there two overall grades, called administrative and executive respectively, but there are eleven grades within these grades, numbered from one down to ten (one grade being subdivided). A successful entrant to the senior, or administrative, grade begins in grade eight (really nine) with the rank of third secretary or vice-consul at a salary of £1,530 a year, and can hope to rise through the ranks of second secretary, first secretary or consul, counsellor or consul-general, assistant under-secretary or minister, to the dizzy heights of deputy under-secretary or head of a grade two mission, and even to the top grade. There are fifteen members of grade one: the permanent under-secretary, who is also head of the Diplomatic Service, and the top ambassadors. Grade two boasts twenty-four ambassadors in what are considered important posts, such as the Republic of Ireland, Malaysia, Belgium, Brazil, Greece, Jordan, Spain; and ten deputy under-secretaries (there was precisely one of these when I entered the Foreign Office in 1935). Then follow the grade three officials: ninety-three abroad, the vast majority of them heads of mission, and eighteen assistant under-secretaries in the Office. Until recently, the new member of the executive grade, who may begin as a vice-consul or junior attaché on the lowest rung, could not seriously hope to rise higher than grade five, in which he could with luck be head of a section, confusingly called a department, in the Office, or of a minor mission abroad. He can now hope for better things.

It is as well to scotch here a persistent diplomatic fiction about embassies and legations. Before the war there were few of the former and they clearly outranked the latter. There is now just one legation in London, representing the Yemen Arab Republic: at the wishes of the smaller and newer countries the others have been 'elevated to the status of embassies'. In practice this means absolutely nothing except that His Excellency the Minister can now call himself His Excellency the Ambassador. His rank and activities and staff remain just the same. Thus it is possible for a British diplomat in as humble a grade as five to be called H.E. the Ambassador; after which he may revert in his next post to the duties and rank of a counsellor or even a first secretary. For traditional reasons, which seem wholly out of date, embassies in Commonwealth countries are called high commissions, and ambassadors high commissioners. This is confusing because in the past some high commissioners in the Empire were in the position of governors. The complicated argument here is that in all Commonwealth countries, except of course in Britain itself, the Queen is represented by a governor-general or governor, and it would be absurd for Her Majesty to dispatch an ambassador to herself. Some high commissioners in London in fact communicate as ambassadors with non-Commonwealth countries.

THE FOREIGN AND COMMONWEALTH OFFICE

The number of departments within the Office, headed by grade four members called counsellors, varies a little from time to time according to variations in the world scene; but at the moment of writing the tally is no less than sixty-six, a meagre reduction on the number existing in the Foreign and Commonwealth Offices when the ministries were separate. It looks like Parkinson's law with a vengeance. They come under three headings: functional, political and administrative. Functional departments cover such things as arms control and disarmament research; aviation, marine and telecommunications; commodities; cultural relations; economists; news; oil; and so on. The political departments are largely geographical—West Indian, near Eastern, eastern European and Soviet, etc.—but also cover such matters as defence policy, 'guidance' (not as sinister as the similarly called organizations in communist countries and Egypt) and planning. Thirdly, there are a number of administrative departments ranging from accommodation, through migration and visa, to three separate personnel departments. Thus the diplomat at home can explore a wide variety of interests, just as he can at posts abroad.

An average department has six to eight members; under the head, one or two assistants of senior first secretary rank, with desk officers below. Most business—drafting telegrams, dispatches, letters, memoranda, answers to parliamentary questions, minutes, and so on—begins at the bottom and works up. If the subject is important enough it goes on and up to the superintending assistant under-secretary or the deputy under-secretary, or even the permanent under-secretary and from there to a minister. But if the subject is simple enough a junior can 'X' it off; while something of the highest urgency or secrecy may never be seen at all in the 'third room', where the juniors sit, or only after action has been taken on it. A disadvantage that has recently developed is the excessive double-banking of assistant and deputy under-secretaries. This tends both to over-complicate decision-making and to narrow too sharply the top of the pyramid where the permanent under-secretary sits in glorious isolation.

MISSIONS ABROAD

A glance at some British missions abroad and some foreign missions here will give a concrete idea of the apparatus in action, though I am here referring only to staff appearing on the official diplomatic list. In Denmark, for instance, apart from the ambassador we have two counsellors, three service attachés, seven first secretaries, three second secretaries, and five others including an archivist and a chaplain—twenty-one in all. Each official has special duties: four commercial, four consular, one information, one labour, one agriculture and food, one culture. In addition, there are five consulates outside Copenhagen. In London, the Danish embassy shows a staff of eighteen, including two ministers, a specialist on multilateral commodity questions and another on fisheries. When we come to Paris our list comprises fifty-seven names, including two ministers, six service attachés and a dozen counsellors. Two members devote themselves to scientific matters. There are a considerable number of consulates outside Paris. The French make do with forty diplomats in London. At Male in the Maldives or Bamako in Mali, on the other hand, our totals are both seven, of whom all are resident elsewhere. The breakdown of Diplomatic Service British-based manpower overseas as a whole shows that the number of, respectively, typists, registry clerks, and those concerned with commerce, politics, and consular work is approximately four hundred in each category. The number of information officers is less than half of each of these.

By way of contrast, the Soviet embassy in London up to the time of the 1971 expulsions numbered eighty-three, against thirty-nine in the British embassy in Moscow. The Soviet diplomat's ranks are specified in a completely traditional diplomatic manner—counsellor, first secretary, etc.—so that except for the service attachés and two trade representatives no hint is given of anyone's special tasks. Egypt has another style again. Of its thirty-five diplomats here—we have just over half as many in Cairo—fifteen are described as 'administrative attachés', a term rarely found in the diplomatic world and no doubt covering a wide variety of duties. Among the sixty-three staff of the United States embassy the only qualifications that are slightly unusual are atomic energy and public affairs. The British embassy in Washington numbers no less than eighty, with as many again in consulates scattered all over the United States. This contrasts with our mere twenty-seven people at the United Nations.

Obviously, and rightly, it is the FCO that co-ordinates and directs our diplomacy, and those officials who reach the ranks of permanent and deputy under-secretary wield a gratifying amount of power. Equally obviously, a man or woman does not go into the Diplomatic Service in order to spend a lifetime in Whitehall. And as we now have thirty-one high commissions in Commonwealth countries, about a hundred embassies, plus seven delegations of similar calibre accredited to international organizations, plus roughly as many again as that combined total in the way of consulates, the opportunities for the individual and the scope of the apparatus are wide indeed. We will consider later whether it is not too wide. In all, well over 3,000 relatively senior UK-based diplomats are serving abroad. One lucky fellow in the lowest executive grade is head of his own small consular post.

These figures include staff concerned with commerce, aid, information, consular matters, registry work, typing, administration, security and communications. But there is a good deal more to the apparatus than that, depending on bodies that are separate from the Diplomatic Service but whose representatives work as part of the apparatus. The British Council provides cultural staff; the Ministry of Defence attachés of all three Services; half a dozen Whitehall departments specialist attachés of various kinds from their own staffs; the Secret Intelligence Service, otherwise known as the Secret Service or DI6, its quota of spies, or spooks; the Security Services, or DI5, security advisers and security liaison officers.

THE FCO'S OFFICIAL GUIDANCE

Though the diplomatic world may appear to be a homogeneous closed shop, there are in fact considerable variations between the methods of functioning of the diplomatic apparatus of different types of nations.

The literature issued to hopeful British candidates shows that as a result of the rationalization, at any rate up to a point, of the British apparatus and the recent surfacing of new men, the atmosphere has become decidedly more contemporary and flexible. The candidate is warned that the grading structure of the Service and the methods of selection are under constant review: this for a start makes a welcome change from the old

Foreign Office List which right up to 1965 included a severe half-page on the protocol laid down at the Congresses of Vienna in 1815 and Aix-la-Chapelle in 1818. The short pamphlet, *Her Majesty's Diplomatic Service*, prepared by the Civil Service Commission and the Central Office of Information, is notably well printed and presented, and pithily written. It states succinctly that the Diplomatic Service is self-contained and that it consists of five branches—the administrative, the executive and clerical, the communications, the secretarial, and the security officer branches respectively. Even in this document, however, some space is unnecessarily devoted to the protocol problems besetting an ambassador's dinner parties; and a diplomat is described as 'above all someone who likes to get things done', with which I fancy human dynamos such as Sir Val Duncan or Sir Arnold Weinstock would hardly agree; and which I myself would describe as, at present, a healthy aspiration but not a *fait accompli*. But on the whole a good practical spirit prevails: the importance of foreign languages is recognized and financial help given to the new entrant to learn them; and he or she will be sent at an early stage to courses in public administration and economics at the Treasury's Centre for Administrative Studies. Members nowadays positively must have an 'understanding of and interest in economic and commercial matters, and social and labour problems, as well as in political questions'. This is a good step forward. Then the method of entry has been rationalized. A good university academic standard is still demanded for the administrative grade—first or second class honours—but the written exam is limited to three papers designed to probe the candidate's common sense, general knowledge and powers of succinct expression; and great weight is laid on the interviews. Social background and type of education are declared to be irrelevant in themselves. In 1970 there were 'about twenty-seven' vacancies for people aged between twenty and twenty-seven; but also, sensibly, limited recruitment to higher grades of suitably qualified candidates between the ages of twenty-seven and forty-four. The general retiring age remains pretty strictly at sixty, though characters who run out of steam can be retired before then and the very occasional man kept on for a year or two beyond.

The good impression made by these FCO publications is

confirmed by the *Diplomatic Service Regulations*, which come in a large and handsome scarlet plastic cover. They comprise some 110 loose-leaf pages, and in practically all cases are literally up to the minute. They are largely concerned, naturally enough, with money: pay, allowances, scales of accommodation, pensions. There is also a good deal about disciplinary matters. Only in one or two matters does an out-of-date attitude seem to hang over. Thus, in an annex to the retirement regulation countries described as Belgian Congo, British Guinea, Persia and Siam appear. The references to the Prevention of Corruption Act and Official Secrets Acts take us back to 1906 and 1911 respectively, showing how essential it is that these and similar acts should be overhauled. I shall have proposals to make at a later stage on the antiquated Official Secrets Acts. 'Speaking in public on matters of national political controversy' is deprecated, though 'participation in parish council affairs is not forbidden to anyone'. The section on uniform smacks of a past age. Here be lace, Russia braid, hats with ostrich feather border, gorgets (though no gussets), plain white pagri, and the detachable gilt spike for the white pith helmet. Here, indeed, is Sir Paul (now Lord) Gore-Booth, all glorious to behold in full colour, modelling the full ambassadorial rig. But most of the compilation is good down-to-earth stuff. Great emphasis is again put on languages. 'Members of the Diplomatic Service are expected, as far as possible, to learn the languages of the country in which they are serving, and to maintain and improve linguistic skills already acquired.' Languages have been carefully classified in accordance with their difficulty, and the rewards in the shape of language allowances scaled accordingly. Thus class 1(a) contains only Amharic, Chinese, Japanese and Korean; 1(b) has seven languages including Arabic and Hebrew; class 2 covers twenty-five, from Albanian to Urdu, and including Russian; and so on.

In a different sphere, the handbook sensibly includes details of the Diplomatic Service Whitley Council and the various unions and associations to which diplomats can belong. The Whitley Council is defined as a joint body consisting of representatives of the 'official side', i.e. the management of the Diplomatic Service, and the 'staff side', i.e. the associations recognized as representing the different categories of staff in the Service. These, in turn, are as follows: the Civil and Public Services Association, covering grade ten and grades two to five of the secretarial branch; the Civil Service Union, for the communications and security officers branches; the Diplomatic Service Association for grades one to eight of the administrative class; the Institution of Professional Civil Servants, for the communications branch again and also for the research cadre and all staff with professional qualifications; and the Society of Civil Servants for the executive class, secretarial branch grade one and Queen's Messengers. The decisions of the Whitley Council are made by agreement between the two sides and are subject to the overriding authority of Parliament and the responsibility of FCO ministers to that body, and the responsibility of the staff side to its constituent associations. An important, and admirable, recent achievement of the Whitley Council, for instance, has been the negotiation of greatly improved superannuation arrangements for the Diplomatic Service, and also improved terms for those 'prematurely retired for management reasons', as the personnel services department nicely puts it. These are modern developments of the organization, and much to be commended from the angle of the contemporary and future morale of the Service. All in all the *Diplomatic Service Regulations* constitutes a well-presented and forward-looking compendium.

Most diplomats will spend approximately two-thirds of their time abroad, and they are expected to go where they are told without demur, whatever family, climatic, health or other problems may threaten to arise; though naturally the personnel authorities are not completely callous in special cases. Tours of duty abroad vary between two and five years in each post, with an average of around three; the same applies to tours in the FCO. A recent innovation is the defining of hours of work in London: normally a five-day week of forty-one hours including lunch intervals. Abroad diplomats are still expected, as they always were, to work the number of hours necessary for the jobs on hand. Those hours can of course vary enormously between busy and slack posts, or busy and slack periods in the same post. The diplomat when abroad is on duty potentially all the time, even when eating or sleeping. I have related how I was roused in the early hours of 13 August 1961 to be told, as I was British

Minister in Berlin, that the East German communists had started
work on the Berlin Wall at 2 a.m. that day, or rather night.

In practice a successful man may well spend his career half and
half at home and abroad: this, for instance, is how the career of
the present Permanent Under-Secretary, Sir Denis Greenhill, is
panning out. The official guidance given on career prospects is
cagey; but this is understandable since, after all, individuals
develop their aptitudes at different speeds and in different directions. Danger points tend to come at around the age of forty and
again at fifty; nevertheless it is possible for a member, probably
worthy but uninspiring, of the administrative grade to rise no
higher than grade five (salary up to nearly £5,000) and yet complete his allotted span, or at least come within two or three years
of it. In the executive grade, as I have said, it is rare for anyone
to rise above grade five. Members of this grade are used on the
same jobs as members of the senior one.

THE CONSULS

Although the former Consular Service is now wholly integrated
in the Diplomatic Service, the picture would be incomplete
without a special reference to our consuls, ranging from quite
grand consuls-general in grade four to proconsuls, often locally
recruited and all the more knowledgeable and useful for that.
The day of the great consuls, who were more in the nature of
imperial proconsuls, is of course past. But there are nearly 200
British consular districts in the world, with senior staffs ranging
from a dozen downwards and junior staffs to match, which carry
out a number of mainly unglamorous but essential duties. Pro-
tection of and assistance to British nationals and their interests is
the broad description of their responsibilities; and in practice
this covers almost everything from commercial and political
reporting to their embassies and to the FCO, to dealing with individuals' problems which may be of a harrowing personal
nature. The consuls have been described as 'the Cinderella service'. The feeling still remains among consular officers in their
fifties who remember the often snobbish attitude of the diplomats proper towards their Service, that they have been hardly
done by. This is the disease known as consularitis, which the
FCO administration is now making a determined effort to cure.

THE SOCIAL ASPECT

An important factor in building a forward-looking British diplomatic apparatus is the social aspect, and this in turn has two sides to it. One is the constitution of the service at and near the top; the other is recruitment. I have criticized in the past the Eton–Winchester stranglehold on the Diplomatic Service; and my criticism has been largely misunderstood. In fact I sent my four sons alternately to these two schools because I thought they provided the best education available. I mention the matter here once more in order to get it out of the way. The point is that the products of these schools who flocked in to the Diplomatic Service until a short time ago were almost all of a conventional, traditional stamp who instinctively took against service in, say, a new African or Asian country, and against the fact that such countries had equal voting power with everyone else in the General Assembly of the United Nations.

There were two further dangers. Many ministers of the Foreign Office and Commonwealth Relations Office, when they were separate, came from the same stable: it was too cosy at the top, too old-boy net by half. Too often there was a smooth consensus on burning questions that fallaciously appeared to take the heat out of them. And in the lower reaches, where grade A descended to grade B (now grade E for executive), and below, there was a good deal of resentment of the social stratification, particularly in posts abroad where total numbers for social purposes were not large. Unfortunately this is not unknown even today.

It is in this sphere that George Brown did so much good. He stood no nonsense from the traditionalists; and it is not surprising that his three public critics among retired ambassadors are one Etonian and two Wykehamists, or that two of his defenders were two un-chic ambassadors of a far more contemporary type. Brown made the unconventional, and successful, appointments of Christopher Soames (an old Etonian, as it happens) to Paris and John Freeman to Washington. He selected Sir Denis Greenhill, a man who stood up to him, from some way down the list as Permanent Under-Secretary. With his advent as head of the Diplomatic Service and the Foreign Office the stranglehold has been broken. Minor public school, work on the railways (though hardly as a ganger), a distinguished fighting war—his record is very different from those of his two predecessors, both old Etonians who had known no life other than that of diplomacy. Nearly all the senior diplomats today have seen life in the forces or elsewhere outside Whitehall; there are even cases where a Mancunian or Scottish accent can be detected, and the Service is all the better for it.

At the recruitment end too matters are improving. A majority of entrants to the administrative grades still come from Oxbridge; but for that matter so do a great many left-wing leaders and thinkers, and it remains a fact that many of the brighter young men and women, from whatever schools, prefer an Oxbridge education. But Michael Stewart made valiant efforts, which are continuing today, to canvass the other universities; and the school origins of candidates today are far wider than they used to be. Thus, where the Plowden report of 1962 showed 94 per cent of the entry to the administrative grades as coming from Oxbridge, in 1971 the figure was 53 per cent to 'redbrick's' 47 per cent. Similarly, in 1971 no less than 70 per cent came from state schools, compared with 28 per cent in 1962. Such people really do find it easier than their predecessors to get on with representatives of the new and the underprivileged countries; and with the lower echelons in our own ranks.

TRANSFERS AND PROMOTIONS

These are nowadays arranged more democratically and less arbitrarily than in the past, though the overriding consideration understandably still obtains: 'In regard to all appointments whatever in the Diplomatic Service, the Secretary of State will be free to make any such selection as he may deem right without being bound by claims founded on seniority or on membership of the Service.' This gives a desirable flexibility to the process.

There are six selection boards which deal with different grades, mainly on the basis of confidential annual reports on the diplomat concerned; and the procedure has been drawn up in agreement with the staff side of the Whitley Council. The senior selection board makes recommendations to the Secretary of State for transfers and promotions in or to grade three or above. Its

chairman is the Permanent Under-Secretary, and it includes two
political ministers as well as other senior officials: a good blend.
The number two selection board is chaired by the chief clerk,
and reports on matters regarding grade four to the Permanent
Under-Secretary; neither this board nor those below it have any
political members. And so on down the line.

Although I think that more rapid promotion for the fliers than
occurs today is desirable, I have no doubt that the system is considerably better than it was. The appointment as ambassador at
Bonn of a career diplomat a mere fifty-three years old, not yet in
grade one, and not yet possessing his 'K' when appointed, is a
hopeful sign. The fact that Niko Henderson has also written a
well-received historical book and various stories and articles in
Penguin New Writing, *Horizon* and *History Today* also shows that
in the diplomatic selection process horizons are widening.[1]

CULTURE

Although the British Council is semi-independent of the FCO, it
naturally works closely with the Diplomatic Service in promoting our interests abroad in the cultural sphere. The cultural relations department of the FCO maintains close liaison with it for
this purpose. Founded in 1934, the Council has a budget of about
£16 million, and the administration of a further £8½ million as
agent for various government departments and international
organizations. It has representatives in some seventy-five countries. In a few of these, where for one reason or another conditions are tricky, they have diplomatic status; but everywhere
they are under instructions to collaborate closely with our diplomatic mission. In its earlier days it was frequently criticized as
arty and ineffectual; but it has by now readjusted its priorities so
as to concentrate on more practical activities and more backward
regions. The Council's main aims are defined as promoting
abroad a wider knowledge of Britain and cultural relations,
which in practice is apt to be a bit woolly; and to develop
English-language teaching, which is an admirable objective, not

---

[1] It is strongly rumoured that one of two very active men aged 51
and 50 respectively will succeed Greenhill as Permanent Under-
Secretary in 1973. This would be all to the good.

least in the developing countries. This it does by sending teachers abroad and welcoming students in London, by running some 200 libraries abroad, by producing English-by-television services overseas, and so on. Its last director-general was an ex-diplomat; but this has never been the case before, and it is no bad thing that his successor is to be a distinguished academic administrator. The reason is that, as with our press, and with broadcasting and television services—whose influence on our diplomacy is very great, but rather outside my sphere at this point—there are advantages in having not only fully official channels through which to operate but also semi-official or entirely unofficial channels too. The director-general's salary is £13,000 a year, only slightly less than that of the head of the Diplomatic Service.

HONOURS

One of the rewards of the successful diplomat is the bestowal of honours by the Sovereign. The Diplomatic Service's own honour is the Most Distinguished Order of St Michael and St George, with its motto 'Token of a better age'. Until the Labour government came to power in 1964 this came with the rations as follows: bright and/or senior counsellors, Companion or CMG (frivolously, 'Call Me God'); all in grades one and two, and some in grades three and four, Knight Commander, or KCMG (Kindly ditto); half a dozen at the very top, Knight Grand Cross or GCMG (God Calls Me God). Occasionally the slightly superior Order of the Bath has been bestowed on diplomats, also in these top ranks, and similarly the Royal Victorian Order on members of a mission in a country which the Queen has visited. One down comes the Most Excellent Order of the British Empire, in four ranks descending to Member: this is largely given to consular officials. Since 1964 the number of awards of all kinds has, sensibly, been far less lavish. It is just possible, though very rare, to reach the top grade as a mister rather than a knight; and you can grace grade two for quite a while without a handle. Since excellent ambassadors from outside the Service made do for some years as Mr Freeman and Mr Soames this can be no great hardship or disadvantage in our day and age. The retiring Permanent Under-Secretary almost always receives a peerage.

THE COST

The cost of the British apparatus is not altogether easy to pin down, as a variety of government departments contribute bits and pieces. The 1971–72 estimates show the Diplomatic Service at some £50 million, Foreign and Commonwealth Services at nearly £24 million, the British Council £9 million (obviously a grave under-estimate); and the Overseas Development Administration £4 million; a total of about £87 million. The Duncan report of 1969, however, puts it rather higher, at some £110 million. About half that sum is in foreign currency; in return a similar sum is spent on foreign representation in Britain. The actual amount of overseas aid dispensed, at some £220 million, does not of course come into my present picture. A considerable proportion of the diplomatic budget—I have no doubt that it is larger than it should be—goes on accommodation. Some of the palatial old embassies in countries which are no longer as important to us as they once were, such as Portugal, demand expensive upkeep which is the responsibility of the Department of the Environment.

SALARIES AND ALLOWANCES

British diplomats employed in London are largely left to their own devices as far as housing and entertaining are concerned, but abroad they are on the whole generously treated. It is not unknown for a modest first secretary in a fortunate post to have a house with a swimming pool. Half a dozen ambassadors receive, in addition to their salaries, tax-free entertainment allowances—pompously called *frais de représentation*—running into five figures annually, and others get lesser but often generous allowances according to the pecking order and the local cost of living. The details of these allowances are not made public, though Parliament does try to keep an eye on them. In a spirited exchange in the House of Commons the Foreign Secretary was asked 'what criteria determined the number of footmen at the British embassy in Washington', and the Parliamentary Under-Secretary replied 'the amount of work involved'. This was greeted with laughter, which changed to 'loud laughter' when he added that he was sure that Lord Cromer had the footmen under control. 'Hospitality,' he said, 'is an important part of the functions of the British ambassador.'

Basic salaries, quite rightly, constantly go up as the cost of living goes up. For the statistically minded I have included (appendix 1) a comparison of salaries at 1 January 1966 and 1969, and 1 July 1972, showing that they now range from £720 per annum to £15,750. They are not bad if you arrive at the top; but not princely either, compared with industry and other occupations. A senior administrative official put it to me this way: the Permanent Under-Secretary's emoluments are nothing much compared with those of the heads of big business; but the rewards for successful people between the ages of thirty-five and fifty are pretty good. My own judgement would be, well, yes and no, particularly as there is still little chance today of meteoric promotion: in 1967 only three officials promoted to grade four were under forty-two, the sort of age at which numerous dynamic executives or journalists, or politicians up and down the country, are at or very near the top and earning very large salaries indeed. There is the modest consolation that, with the great proliferation of independent countries, the chances of a promising young diplomat being put in charge of a post at an earlier age than he would have been in the past are appreciably heightened. And at such a post he may well have the useful experience of dealing personally with a head of state or foreign minister, however humble his own rank may be.

Compared with our defence expenditure of nearly £3,000 million, then, the cost of the diplomatic apparatus is a fleabite; nevertheless the real cost today of £120 million is a serious sum of money and we have a right to assure ourselves that the apparatus gives good value in return. Yes, but good value for what? It is not very profitable to keep on staring at an apparatus in the void. The answer is: for the purpose of achieving our diplomatic objectives in the 1970s, which I have already tried to define. I shall attempt later to assess the adequacy of the apparatus for the task demanded of it.

CHAPTER SEVEN

To see ourselves . . .

The first essential of good diplomacy is to know what the country, or the international organization, with which you are dealing really thinks: thinks about your own side, and thinks about itself. Next comes a stringently objective assessment, and constant reassessment, of your own side's capabilities. Only after these come the subtleties and stratagems which used to be generally regarded as 'diplomacy', and by many people still are. These consist of nuances, of deliberate overstatements here and understatements there, of friendly or less friendly relations, of crafty negotiations, of propaganda, of deception operations. All of these can be useful as long as they are deliberately executed, with a cool head, in the light of what goes before. The diplomatic apparatus must be designed, year in year out, to cope with these various facets.

The Duncan report made a good fist of planning the apparatus for the 1970s, but the conditions in which it worked had certain disadvantages. It was working against time, and in fact could not find time to discuss matters with many foreigners; it was under orders to produce economies, which is of course a good thing, but which can prove inhibiting in some directions; it was not dealing with the nerve centre of our diplomatic apparatus, the FCO.

On the first of my categories above, light is thrown not only by discussions with British and foreign diplomats of a variety of ranks but also by a wide-ranging series of recent books and other expressions of opinion. There is Herman Kahn, head of the Hudson Institute with its powerful think-tank techniques, dealing not only with the terrifying possibilities of thermo-nuclear diplomacy but, equally seriously, with the state of the world in 'The Year 2000'. There are the highly distinguished American diplomats George Kennan and George W. Ball. There are the retired British diplomats, including the best of his generation, Lord Trevelyan, and the academic cold warrior Sir William Hayter. Another of these, in a rather special category, sends us the message from Moscow: the traitor Donald Maclean. There is a revealing recent opinion poll from Japan. I shall attempt, by taking a balanced selection of views expressed by these various authorities, to pinpoint some of the strengths and weaknesses of recent British diplomacy, and hence to indicate its potential for the future. None of my sources is 'anti-British', except Donald Maclean, but they vary widely and productively in their estimates and criticisms.

Dean Acheson's famous remark in 1962 that Britain had lost an empire and not yet found a role had a traumatic effect here for several reasons. First and foremost, it was so clearly true and to the point. Secondly, many British people refused to face the fact that our imperialist days are over; some dream neo-imperialist dreams even now, ten years later. Thirdly, many relied on the comfortable cushioning effect of a 'special relationship' with the United States, which in reality has become less and less special over recent years and will never again become what it was during most of the second world war. Finally, American statesmen and diplomats usually express themselves most politely on the subject of Britain's position in the world, however wholeheartedly they may agree with Acheson's dictum. It is worth quoting the relevant passage from Acheson's speech more fully:

> Great Britain has lost an empire and has not yet found a role. The attempt to play a separate power role—that is, a role apart from Europe, a role based on being the head of a 'commonwealth' which has no political structure, or unity, or strength, and enjoys a fragile and precarious economic relationship by means of the sterling area and preferences in the British market—this role is about played out.

Ten years later we can at least say that an honest attempt is being made by Britain to play a profitable new role, in the European Communities.

THE VIEWS OF GEORGE W. BALL

Acheson was certainly not anti-British; he was indeed disliked by some of his American colleagues on the grounds that his style and manners were too much like those of an old-world English gentleman. George W. Ball, who in 1967 wrote *The Discipline of Power: Essentials of a modern world structure*, is positively pro-British and has worked together most amicably with British ministers of both parties and with British diplomats. Though not known to the general public here, he was Under-Secretary of State for over six years with Presidents Kennedy and Johnson, and then US ambassador to the United Nations. He shows in his book that one of his dearest wishes is to see Britain exercise the influence she should in the world; yet clearly he agrees with Acheson's criticisms. He goes on to propose policies which will be resented by many people here; indeed, it would be fair to say by the majority of newspaper readers, who are innately conservative-minded and who do not give much deep thought to our international relations anyway. 'In these days,' he remarks, 'there is a great deal of talking and writing about foreign policy, but there can never be too much, since there is an insatiable need for fresh insights and new appraisals.' That is his attitude; and in point of fact the new policies that he suggests for Britain are very sensible.

Two of Ball's central chapters are called 'The Special Problem of the UK' and, quite baldly, 'The Disadvantages of the Special Relationship'. He gets his priorities right: nuclear factors top, economic second, political and diplomatic only third. The results of the interaction of the factors are quite simply that there are two super-powers and that it is hopeless for Britain, or any other nation with the possible exception of China in the future, to attempt to compete. (He could be wrong in not including Japan and, let us hope, the EEC.) 'Only a cohesive society with a population approaching 200 million and a national income of at least $300 billion can claim a commanding position of world power.' It is precisely Britain's misguided efforts since the war to assert such a claim that have hastened her decline. In the nuclear sphere she has wasted large quantities of money and manpower, first in clawing her way up the nuclear ladder, and secondly in insisting on having the Polaris deterrent, which no longer is one. Here Ball blames the 'special relationship' and the US government's weakness in pandering to Britain's delusions about it.

He analyses deeply three specific occasions on which US policy would have been better for everyone had it been cruel to be kind. These were the 1958 liberalizing amendments of the MacMahon Act; the generous offer in 1960 of the Skybolt missile, which proved a failure; and the compensatory offer at Nassau in 1962 of Polaris. 'By pressing Polaris submarines on the British, we made possible the unedifying spectacle of a Britain that clings to a nuclear deterrent which she cannot afford, which, by itself, has no realistic military value, and which has got into the way of her entry into Europe.' Into the bargain, 'wherever the US and the UK join together in a common enterprise, decisions are distorted by the disparity in the resources that each nation can command'. He hopes to God that the US government will not make a fourth blunder by acceding to any British requests for up-to-date nuclear weapons, for instance Poseidon or other multiple-warhead missiles.

In the non-nuclear sphere Ball thinks that the US government has been irresponsible in encouraging Britain, with her Kipling-esque dreams of East of Suez, to keep large forces in south-east Asia long after they served any useful purpose there, and at a time when the savings on their expensive deployment could have been used to so much better effect nearer home. This state of affairs at any rate has been remedied by now.

Ball's positive recommendations for Britain's future policy are as acute as his criticisms of the past. First, she must abandon all pretensions to nuclear status; the considerable resources now diverted to nuclear matters could then be devoted to shoring up her ailing economy. Also, this would be a most helpful gesture in the context of the vitally needed prevention of proliferation. Second, Britain must also give up unwarranted pretensions in the economic sphere, for instance in connection with the position of sterling and her relations with the Commonwealth. Once again, cutting her coat according to the cloth available would profoundly benefit her economy. This must go along with fundamental changes in the attitudes of labour and management so that the British economy can become efficient by contemporary, and future, standards. Third, and intimately bound up with both the economic and political spheres, Britain must work whole-heartedly within Europe. Not only would this benefit her economically in the long run; it would also give her a political sphere commensurate with her capabilities. More than this, a combined Europe—Ball is not too clear on whether some communist-ruled states should eventually be included if possible —would form a third power which, except in the nuclear sphere, could look the super-powers in the eye. A united western Europe, to a large extent led by Britain, could have a truly special relationship with the US, if it made up its mind to it. And it would be easier for the world to balance on three wheels rather than two. He disagrees with Senator Fulbright that the US, or for that matter the USSR, too often uses its power arrogantly; but at the same time the temptation to do so would be less if a sound, powerful, rich and populous Europe existed. The very fact that Ball wants to see Britain play her proper part makes him want to see her less, and not more, dependent on the US. Ball also discusses the alternative possibility of a federation of the United States, Canada, Britain, Australia and New Zealand, and rightly comes down against it. I find it hard to fault Ball on his friendly suggestions for increasing Britain's diplomatic in-fluence in the world. Both in the US and here, he is very much the contemporary diplomat's diplomat.

In other books by distinguished Americans about world affairs which have appeared in the last few years the attitude towards Britain is similar. Senator J. William Fulbright, in *The Arrogance of Power*, is kindly and certainly not condescending; but he firmly puts her in her place, beta plus or II(1) in the exam honours list. George Kennan, one of the US's most able career diplomats ever, in his *Memoirs 1925–50*, devotes relatively little space to Britain and simply does not mention several of her leaders, such as Attlee, Eden and Macmillan. As regards the post-war period, she is for him a sort of problem child, always needing extensive assistance from the US and growing up obstinately slowly.

HERMAN KAHN

A clinical approach is taken by Herman Kahn, generally known as the 'doomsday man' because he indulges in—to quote the title of one of his books—'thinking about the unthinkable'. This mathematician and physicist has for years been pondering and writing about the full implications of thermo-nuclear policy and strategy, with the supreme purpose of showing how, in spite of any and all possible provocations, a thermo-nuclear holocaust can be avoided; or, if the worst comes to the worst, its frightful results kept within some bounds. His work has had a great influence on the US government's policies over the biggest crises. President Kennedy's adroit handling of the Berlin Wall crunch in 1961–62 and of the Cuba missile confrontation later in 1962 resembled a playing out of one of Kahn's most sophisticated 'scenarios'. It is a fact that his work has been studied in the Kremlin; it has no doubt helped to avoid the spilling over of the tensions of the cold war, extreme as they have been, into hot war itself. Paradoxically if you wish, his minutely careful analysis of all the possibilities and implications has had a restraining effect on the Soviet government.

Kahn's three books about thermo-nuclear policy naturally enough give little space to Britain's capabilities and problems in that sphere. In his more general one, *The Year 2000: A framework for speculation on the next thirty-three years*, published in 1967 in collaboration with Anthony J. Wiener, he makes a very serious attempt to forecast the state of the world strategically, economically and politically during the years up to the end of this century, employing to the full the better think-tank techniques. Many of his statistical extrapolations are highly significant for international relations during this period, and although Britain receives no special attention they are significant for our own foreign policy and hence our diplomacy. In the nuclear sphere he reckons that Britain, France and West Germany seem to be about ten to fifteen years behind the US in central war technology. This means that by, say, 1975 they could, if they spent enough money, stand about where the US stood in 1960. He is too kind to underline the fact that this would be totally futile. Economically, Britain and France have, relatively, been declining since 1900, while the US, the USSR, Germany and Japan have been rising, though with fearful temporary setbacks in the case of the last three. Of the seven super and large powers, Britain's gross national product in 1966 came fourth, near that of West Germany, France and Japan; but by 1980 he estimates that it will have sunk to sixth, ahead only of China who will probably overtake her in the following fifteen years. Another intriguing calculation is that Britain would need nineteen years from 1965 to reach the United States' GNP in that year, coming below France (18 years), East Germany (17), West Germany (16), Canada (12) and, top of the list, Sweden (11). Just below Britain are Czechoslovakia, Japan, Israel and Australia. A good deal less fortunate are Egypt, Thailand and China, all needing around 100 years. At the bottom of the table Nigeria is calculated to require 339 years, Colombia 358, and the wretched Indonesia 593. Another calculation shows the US, Japan, Canada, Scandinavia, Switzerland, France, West Germany and Benelux in the 'visibly post-industrial' phase by the year 2000; while Britain, the USSR, Italy, Austria, East Germany, Czechoslovakia, Israel, Austria and New Zealand come into the second league, called 'early post-industrial'. However, he does not categorize the expanded EEC as such. Relevant too is the forecast that the growth rate of Britain's population of 55 million in 1965 is likely to be nil for the foreseeable future. Only West Germany's after 1985 is equally inactive.

Kahn's chapter on international politics in the standard world attempts in straightforward fashion to predict nuclear, economic and political developments up to the year 2000; it seems to me that ten or fifteen years ahead might be more practical. In a sense Kahn thinks so too, for his following chapter, called 'Some Canonical Variations from the Standard World', spreads its tentacles in a more elaborate fashion. Under three main headings—'more integrated'; 'more inward-looking'; and 'greater disarray' —come some suggestive subheadings. Under the first: 'relatively peaceful, prosperous, arms-controlled worlds . . . (1) Stability or *status quo* oriented, (2) Development or aid-oriented.' Under the second: 'Worlds that are almost as peaceful and prosperous, but with little arms control or general co-ordination . . . (3) with an eroded communist movement, (4) with an eroded democratic morale and some communist dynamism, (5) with a dynamic Europe and/or Japan.' Finally, under 'greater disarray . . . relatively troubled and violent worlds, but in which no large central wars have occurred', considered under the same subheadings as (3), (4) and (5). And, logically enough, this chapter is followed by two on 'some possibilities for nuclear wars' and 'other twenty-first century nightmares'.

All this may seem rather a far cry from diplomacy and the diplomatic apparatus. But I believe, on the contrary, that intelligent estimates such as these should be considered in connection with our foreign policy and diplomacy, and hence with the shape and development of our diplomatic apparatus. The particular importance of Kahn is, precisely, that alone among the authorities I am quoting in this chapter he has never had a professional connection with diplomacy; this position outside the daily hurly-burly may well have given him more rather than less influence on its global charisma than the deeply involved professionals can exercise. On Britain's economic and political situation as such Kahn has not much to say. He points out that while Britain is gently sliding down the competitive scale, or 'decaying' as he calls it, most of her inhabitants have 'never had it so good' and continue to have it even better. 'If current trends continue, before the year 2000 England will have fallen from the richest of the five large powers'—and in some ways this was true as late as 1955—'to the poorest, even while its GNP has quintupled.' He observes that she may or may not join the EEC; but that in any case the EEC is unlikely to attain the cohesion of another United States.

DONALD MACLEAN

I turn now to a source well worthy of consideration on the opposite side of the fence. In a wry fashion we can be grateful for Donald Maclean, at one time a very up-and-coming British diplomat who betrayed numerous top secrets of his country and of the US to the communists for many crucial years up to 1951, when on his fellow-traitor Philby's warning of imminent exposure he skipped to Moscow with his like-minded friend Burgess. As he puts it, with a rare glint of wit in his foreword to *British Foreign Policy since Suez*, first published in Britain in 1970:

'After having spent the first sixteen years of my working life in the Diplomatic Service, I found myself faced with the necessity of finding a new profession'. The book is written in a style which combines cold Marxist analysis with British officialese. It has deluded some people by its apparent reasonableness. It is true that much of the analysis, both of the past and of trends for the future, is to the point: he is quoted by one of our top ambassadors in the lead-in to his latest book on the Middle East. But reading between the lines reveals his relish at the decline of British power, his hatred of American power and influence, his divisive aims where Anglo-American collaboration is concerned, and naturally his firm faith that the 'socialist' part of the world is the world of the future.

It is tempting to conclude that his judgements can all be stood on their heads; but the matter is more subtle than that. After all, the communist half of the world exists and flourishes; and as he remarks in the only other witticism that I could find in the book, 'the only alternative to peaceful co-existence was and is peaceful non-existence'. Thus, though the work is propaganda, albeit of a reasonably sophisticated kind, it can help us in our quest to see ourselves as others see us. Like George Ball he has chapters on the 'special relationship' and the decline of British influence. Also like Ball and Kahn, he gets the foreign policy priorities correct: nuclear power, economic strength, political and diplomatic adroitness.

He begins with the usual crop of statistics comparing Britain's economic performance with that of the other large powers and the US, though never with the USSR. He soon reaches the desirable conclusion, from the communist point of view, that 'twilight is falling on Western unity'. In reality that is more than doubtful; as is his theme that the US has throughout hampered Britain's entry into Europe. His picture of Britain dithering in the past and for the future between 'a transatlantic and cross-channel orientation' is a gross misrepresentation. He tries, vainly, to make out that Harold Wilson, when Prime Minister, echoed de Gaulle's anti-Americanism. He strongly supports the various suggestions by Rapacki, Gaitskell and others over the years since 1957 to reduce tension in central Europe, and criticizes the unreality of the attitude of the West to East Germany. Here I agree with him that much more could have been done on our side, and this should be one of our main preoccupations in the 1970s, especially as Chancellor Willy Brandt is doing so much to create a more favourable atmosphere. Maclean cautiously observes that the 'special relationship' is 'now possibly nearing its end', especially as it had been based since the end of the war on anti-communism, which was now itself tending to be diluted. He opines that 'the Anglo-American common front, constructed with such difficulty and effort, may, it seems to me, before long begin to crumble'. In general he is obsessively anti-British and anti-American, though he foresees Britain exercising more influence in Europe in the 1970s. On nuclear matters he makes the sound point that Britain 'cannot claim a place at Soviet–American discussions on the question of anti-ballistic missile systems, because she has not the resources to build such a system, nor does the US require British territory or British assistance to build its own'. Also: 'Britain has an advanced modern industry and first-class scientists and technologists, but not on a scale to sustain the cracking pace of the contemporary arms race without going bankrupt.'

Maclean regards as sensible the British withdrawal from Aden, south-east Asia and the Persian Gulf, but warns that 'ultra-colonialism is not dead'. He judges that British asseverations of loyalty to SEATO and CENTO, originally set up in the Dulles era as anti-communist alliances, are mere lip-service and futile today. He considers in general that the British are likely to abandon progressively the rigid anti-communist attitudes of the cold war at its height. I would not disagree with him on any of these points. As regards Africa south of the Sahara, with the exception of the South African and Rhodesian Republics, he sees Britain as predominant in most spheres—industrial, financial, agricultural, training of civil servants and police, teaching; here the US influence is far behind, and he believes we can hold our leading position in the future. I hope he is right. He points out the dangers of any weakness towards the two white minority-dominated countries. He thinks that in south-east Asia we should be able to remain at least 'half in and half out' for some time, thanks to our economic and political links. So, as regards the third world as a whole, he sees southern Africa as 'the only recognizable predominantly British sphere of influence' in the 1970s, while that influence fades away more or less rapidly elsewhere.

Maclean's conclusions are reasonably constructive. Britain has had to lower her sights and must continue to do so; but if this is skilfully achieved the decline of her power compared with that of 'the other leading capitalist states' might well be reversed in the seventies and eighties. For one thing she should reduce the proportion of her GNP spent on military activities to at least the corresponding figure for France and West Germany. She would also do well to join them in the Common Market—though part of Maclean's motive here is to forestall a North Atlantic grouping. He makes a good point when he says that 'the error factor in foreign policy has been so big as substantially to influence the course of events for the worse'. He tracks it down to nostalgia, euphoria and wishful thinking; and on this point again I believe he is right. He doubts whether the senior generation of British diplomats can grasp the consequences for diplomacy of the scientific and technological revolution that is gathering momentum. Stanford University in California has, after all, calculated that the sum of human knowledge—admittedly a rather broad concept—doubled between 1800 and 1900, then again between 1900 and 1950, then in the following ten years, and yet again between 1960 and 1966. So contemporary diplomats, like other human beings, will have to run at a furious pace even to stand still. In sum, Maclean provides ample food for thought by those responsible for British diplomacy over the next fifteen years.

ALEXANDER DRENKER

So, in a different style, does the recently retired West German diplomat, Alexander Drenker, in his book *Diplomaten ohne Nimbus!*, which title he explains should be understood to mean 'Away with the diplomat's halo'. Quite apart from the special German problem of forming a new Service after the defeat without including too many ex-nazis, he considers that the West German Diplomatic Service is still too pompous, too fond of gold braid, too snobbish, too backward-looking. 'Close as we now are to the twenty-first century, we have not even advanced altogether beyond the nineteenth.' There is too much difference between the insiders and the outsiders. In his opinion far too much time is wasted on political reporting by small and middle-sized embassies: it could be cut by two-thirds and no harm done. He quotes State Secretary Günther von Hase, press chief to two Chancellors and now ambassador in London, as saying that he learnt more from the press than from the diplomats, who often passed on press reports and views at second hand and more slowly than their originators. More thought should be given, too, to the influence of television on diplomacy in today's world. Are career diplomats necessarily more reliable than other people, he asks. The US got along well enough without a career Foreign Service until after the first world war, and without allowing career diplomats to head embassies until 1946. A new style of diplomacy, and hence diplomat, is required, thanks to the pro-liferation of international multilateral bodies: he quotes the 1967 *Yearbook of International Organizations* as listing 2,134 of these, 174 being inter-state. West Germany belonged to 129 of them. For many such bodies experts and specialists were re-quired, rather than all-round diplomats of the traditional cut. Even a straightforward embassy such as that of the United States in London contained in 1964 representatives of forty-four ministries and agencies. The large number of developing coun-tries also call for a more contemporary type of diplomat: East Germans often proved more successful in this direction than those from the West. He quotes statistics showing that, in spite of all the foreseeable aid to be given to developing countries by the richer countries, the gap between the two groups will in-exorably increase as the years go by. He calls for more specialized training in the administration of aid; and emphasizes the greatly increased importance of advanced training in a wide variety of languages. He considers that the British and French Diplomatic Services vie with each other for the title of the world's best; and he admires the French system, under which the ablest graduates of the Ecole Nationale d'Administration can rise meteorically in the government service. He praises the Fulton report as forward-looking; and he concedes, approvingly, that the Brandt govern-ment is undertaking a broadening of the base, and a general

shake-up, of the West German diplomatic apparatus. In his esti-
mation the numbers in the West German Foreign Office and
Diplomatic Service could with advantage be 'almost halved'.

Several of these criticisms and suggestions are worth consider-
ing in connection with the improvement of the British diplomatic apparatus. To complete for the moment our survey of how
others see us, I offer brief quotes from the late Chancellor
Adenauer, and from a recent Japanese opinion poll, as if anyone
took opinion polls seriously anyway. Cantankerous old Adenauer
handed down the following judgement: 'The British have no
particular urge to work. After they were thrown out of northern
France, they turned to trading and colonizing, and acquired an
easy way of life—different from the hard work that is the style on
the Continent. They are still at it.' As for the leading Japanese
businessmen and financiers who were polled, their modest
opinion, as to 40 per cent, was that their own nation was
'superior' in the world; the West Germans received 30 per cent
of votes, the Americans 17 per cent, and the British and French
2 per cent each.

It is time to turn to the recently expressed opinions of two
eminent British diplomats on the possibilities and requirements
of our diplomacy.

SIR WILLIAM HAYTER

Sir William Hayter's short book on *Russia and the World* published in 1970 is, I fear, an object lesson on how not to conduct
diplomacy in the 1970s. After a brilliant career in which he became ambassador in Moscow at the age of forty-seven, and
number two in the Office at fifty-one, he decided to give up diplomacy and a year later, in 1958, became Warden of New College,
Oxford. It is all too clear that his ideas derive from the cold war
at its bitterest, in which he was involved at a high level. The
blurb on the dust jacket is ominous, for a start. The Soviet
Union is said to consider that 'permanent hostility to the world
at large is not only justified, but inevitable'. This seems to leave
out of the calculation the hundreds of millions of inhabitants of
communist, and neutralist, states throughout the world. Hayter
sets the tone when he refers to the Soviet Union and her friends
as being states 'in which there is no rule of law'. He might as well

have gone the whole hog and called them Kipling's 'lesser breeds without the law'. In general he attempts to view the USSR *de haut en bas*; which is not convincing when you are writing about one of the two undoubted super-powers from your own less elevated position. He remarks that Brezhnev and Kosygin are 'faceless people', whereas in reality they and their policies are clearly known to millions of people, and indeed admired by them. Most of our own leaders are far more faceless. He sees fit to remark that Soviet leaders tend to be 'shortish'—he does not actually specify nasty and brutish as well—and not very well dressed. They base their policy deliberately on 'untruthfulness', and are incapable of learning the facts of international life. If that were so it must be said that they have achieved a remarkable degree of influence in their ignorant state. Many of his criticisms could apply equally in the West: for instance, the intelligence organization is sometimes taken by surprise; it has its own channels between the head office and embassies abroad; few of the Politburo, equivalent in this respect to our Cabinet, have any special knowledge of foreign affairs; the diplomats themselves do not have much influence over policy.

On the 1968 invasion of Czechoslovakia Hayter takes the stock line, manifesting a sudden and surprising love for a certain group of communists, carefully selected of course as being against the main trend of communism. He does not mention that the CIA were very ready over the months to exploit the situation in an anti-Soviet sense if matters ran their way. Nor does he record that the behaviour of many West Germans, of the type of the ex-nazi Chancellor Kiesinger, was decidedly provocative.

When he turns to East Germany, Hayter is highly unrealistic. 'This is the weakest link in Russia's east European chain': in fact it has the highest standard of living of any communist country and, with just over seventeen million inhabitants, is the fifth most powerful industrial state in Europe. It is 'despotically ruled by quislings': in fact the long-established Ulbricht has for years been respected as an elder statesman in the communist world, and there is nothing despotic about Erich Honecker or Willi Stoph. The thesis that 'if Soviet support for Ulbricht were withdrawn, the adherence of East to West Germany would follow almost automatically', is pure wishful thinking. As regards the

USSR's increasing involvement in the Middle East, which is of great significance and adds a new dimension to her foreign policy, Hayter has little to say.

Given that so much of Hayter's analysis is subjective and inaccurate, it is not surprising that his conclusions are purely negative. The West can only be patient and 'sit tight' for 'there are no solutions'. Some day 'new men' will rule in the Kremlin. There is not a word about the Rapacki plan or its successors. This sort of diplomacy, especially as advocated by honest and very able men like Hayter, did Britain harm enough in the 1950s and 1960s, as is plain for all to see. It goes without saying that similar attitudes would be entirely inappropriate in facing the problems of the 1970s.

LORD TREVELYAN

Thus Hayter sets out to describe what the diplomacy of today and tomorrow should be, but succeeds only in repeating the ideas of the day before yesterday. Lord Trevelyan, in *The Middle East in Revolution*, does not set out any guidelines for the future; but his crisp, no-nonsense account of his activities at three almost impossibly difficult posts gives us an admirable model for the truly contemporary diplomat. On his arrival in Cairo as ambassador in August 1955, he warned the FO that it was futile to act as if the West had the monopoly of supplying arms to Egypt: within a few weeks the Czechoslovak, that is to say Soviet, deal was done. He also warned that the good effects of the 1954 Anglo-Egyptian agreement to withdraw British troops by mid-1956 were wearing very thin: he was soon proved right again. On some mildly anti-British propaganda at one stage he comments: 'I must confess that in Cairo we saw little in these articles of special note. The British government did not take that view. The British press whipped up a campaign against Nasser in reply. He was public enemy number one. We should use the old gun-boat diplomacy and make him give in. All this built up Nasser's status as an Arab leader.' This was indeed the road to Suez. Trevelyan kept his cool throughout, and maintained as good relations as were possible with Nasser. His wife got on well with Madame Nasser; she was the first Englishwoman ever to meet her.

The moment that Nasser nationalized the Canal at the end of July 1956, Eden and Selwyn Lloyd gave three of us in the FO, of whom I was one, top secret instructions to prepare with the Chiefs of Staff a plan to remove Nasser by force. Trevelyan was never told this. However, as rumours were flying about, he commented to London: 'Nasser would fight if attacked and would block the Canal. It should not be difficult to defeat the Egyptian forces, but the difficulties would start after that.' He learnt of the Anglo-French ultimatum from the ticker-tape. 'I found that if I had been ignored, so had practically the whole of the Foreign Office.' He roundly condemns, but without bitterness, the idiocy of the whole conception and the counterproductive futility of its execution. Thanks to his diplomacy the large British community, which was wholly abandoned by Eden to Nasser's mercy, was not savaged. When he returned to London he found that ministers were 'too busy' to see him; but the Queen was not. He considered quitting the Service; fortunately for the Service he did not.

In July 1958 the King of Iraq and members of his family were assassinated, together with the pro-British Prime Minister and various others. The British Embassy was burnt and looted, and the ambassador of the day was attacked. In December Trevelyan arrived to make what he could of the shambles of Anglo-Iraqi relations. He soon realized that the dictator Qasim was a maniac. But 'our policy should be neither to support nor to oppose him, but to do business with him so long as he remained in power, if we could'. Through appalling difficulties of every kind Trevelyan achieved just that. Clearly in constant danger of being assassinated, he kept cool, cheerful and businesslike throughout. He stuck it out until 1961, when Qasim gave him a farewell banquet, and told him how much he appreciated his work as ambassador and his personal relations with the government. In different Iraqi circles it was rumoured that Trevelyan had had Qasim in his pocket, had planned to have him murdered, and was himself a communist agent. His mild comment is: 'Some Arabs will believe anything'. He ends with an affectionate tribute to the 'warm-hearted Iraqi people'.

After well-earned retirement following a successful spell as ambassador in Moscow, Trevelyan was hauled back in 1967 to clear up the appalling mess created in Aden by a long list of governors, high commissioners, generals and the rest. By his usual dynamic and businesslike methods he did so in seven months, with a relatively light tally of casualties. Soon after arrival: 'At last the constitution was agreed. By that time, it was irrelevant. I refused to take the trouble of reading it.' He had to negotiate with rival groups of Adenis who killed each other with as much zest as they killed the British. But: 'We had to stick to the decision to withdraw. We were not going to create a little Vietnam.' Showing patience, firmness and great personal courage he persisted in his efforts to create some sort of order out of chaos, in spite of the maddening behaviour of the Adenis themselves. He expressed gratitude to Foreign Secretary George Brown, 'who had backed us through all our crises and had an imaginative grasp of the situation'. As time marched on he issued a statement 'that we should soon be ready to leave and that the groups should come to a quick decision. This statement had no effect whatsoever.' The FO still stickled that the National Liberation Front, the most powerful of the groups, must ask directly for negotiations. 'We did not see it in this way. It was by now obvious that we only had the choice to hand over to the NLF or to nobody. . . . It was one of those situations which look completely different at either end.' And finally: 'On 29 November the last British troops left. It all happened in perfect peace. We had acted as it suited us and had never given in to pressure from political groups inside and outside the country. We left without glory but without disaster. Our period of occupation did the country little permanent good. Whatever was to come after us, the time for us to be there was over.'

This is the type of realistic and courageous thinking, and active diplomacy, which we shall continue to need in the seventies and beyond. Trevelyan had served in the Indian Civil Service until he was forty-two. Not for him the fashionable diplomatic posts; he tackled a series of the most difficult problems going. He never hesitated to tell the FO where he thought its judgement mistaken; equally, he was never contumacious, and having received his final instructions he got ahead with the job. He acknowledged that in certain situations there was little positive that British diplomacy could achieve; but he was always ferreting around to discover some new angle of approach that might produce results. His achievements show that in diplomacy it is better to be realistic than over-optimistic or over-pessimistic; active rather than passive; tough rather than smooth.

CHAPTER EIGHT

Some Foreign Apparatuses

THE UNITED STATES

The United States diplomatic apparatus is radically different from the British for a number of reasons: its history; the scale and nature of its commitments; the multiplicity of powerful government departments and agencies that dictate—often conflicting—policies. And beyond that again, there is the enormous power and day-to-day influence of bodies which are largely beyond the government's control: Congress on the one hand, and on the other the world's biggest industrial complex, with its particularly close ties with the military.

First, I must declare my own interest. Unlike many of my compatriots who, while professing great admiration for the Americans, deep down envy them, resent their power and influence, and take every opportunity of criticizing and denigrating them, I am a convinced admirer of their achievements in the commercial, military, diplomatic and cultural spheres. I have even been accused by a friend in the CIA of being too kind about the conduct of their foreign affairs in my writings. Admittedly, a people that achieves great things in a good cause, such as rescuing us in the second world war and, more recently, our interests in the Middle East, is capable of gigantic blunders too, such as Vietnam.

If the British Diplomatic Service has been over-revered in the past, and perhaps still is up to a point, the reverse is true of the US Foreign Service. President Truman wrote, not so very long ago: 'Protocol and striped pants give me a pain in the neck'; and the striped-pants cookie-pusher loomed large in *Call Me Madam*. It is difficult to imagine similar sentiments being expressed in Buckingham Palace, No. 10, or the upper reaches of Whitehall. The US Foreign Service only came into being in 1924; and until the second world war it had to operate on the understanding that diplomacy itself was a disgraceful, machiavellian pastime of the decadent 'old world'. As a concomitant of the disturbance in the world power structure caused by the war, a revolution in diplomacy came about: down in influence went the diplomatic services of Britain, France and others—though they were slow to realize the degree of the decline—and up, willy-nilly, those of the US and the USSR. President Truman did much to foster the progress of a career service which could and did handle, with increasing efficiency, every sort of problem, world-wide. Reasonable salaries were paid to members of the Foreign Service, instead of the laughable sums doled out before.

Before the second world war there were some 700 Foreign Service officers serving in Washington and abroad; now the tally is some 4,500—still lower than the corresponding British figure. However, there are in addition, on an official estimate, some tens of thousands of employees of government and private organizations working on foreign problems. The larger missions are conglomerates, unlike the homogeneous groups of diplomatic specialists of yesteryear. The numbers vary greatly: a total of four in Burundi; sixty-odd in Venezuela, of whom only eight belong to the executive and political sections; some 600 in London, about half of them British; about 900 in Afghanistan, mostly construction personnel with the Agency for International Development (AID), but with considerable responsibilities for good relations none the less. There is less and less call for the Ugly American; though the sometimes sinister Quiet American still flourishes in certain quarters.

The annual written competition for entry as Foreign Service officers of the Department of State or as Foreign Service information officers of the US Information Agency calls for as broad a recruitment base as possible. Starting salaries may be as much as $10,000; the eventual salary of the class one officer at something over $35,000 seems distinctly less generous in comparison. As in our Diplomatic Service, there are in addition various allowances for quarters, cost of living, hardship posts, education of children and so on. Much emphasis is laid on economic and commercial reporting. The USIA is a powerful semi-independent service; far more importance is attributed to its propaganda and cultural activities than to those of the British information services and the British Council. Candidates are of course checked for security; and spouses must be US citizens. The examination can be taken at any of about 300 towns in the US, and also at any American diplomatic or consular post abroad—a decidedly broader spread than is available to the British candidate. Each successful candidate has to be approved by the Senate.

One hangover from the Foreign Service's less prestigious days is the custom of making political appointments to many ambassadorial posts. Although far more career diplomats reach the top today than twenty years ago, it is the accepted custom that plum jobs still go to those who have rendered party political services, usually, to put it bluntly, in the shape of large sums of hard cash. Such is the case of the present US ambassador in London, Walter Annenberg; and try as I may I can find few, if any, Americans, whether inside the Service or not, who have a word to say in favour of his diplomatic performance. And I quote a *Daily Express* report on a possible successor: 'America's highest contributor to the Republican Party cause is strongly tipped to replace present US ambassador Walter Annenberg. He is sixty-eight-year-old W. Clement Stone, small, pudgy, with an old-fashioned waxed moustache. He supported President Nixon with one million dollars in last year's [i.e. 1968's] election campaign. "If a family has wealth in the neighbourhood of 400 million dollars, what's a million in gifts?" asks Mr Stone blandly. "Money is power. Money is good." '

But we may ask whether money necessarily makes a good diplomat; and it is fairly easy to supply the answer. The irrepressible Professor Galbraith has written frankly of 'irrelevance in Regent's Park', with reference to the US ambassador's palace there. 'No Englishman,' he says, 'however retarded, would form his view of the United States from the American ambassador and change it with each new one. . . . The American ambassador is an anachronism, kept alive between the occupant of the post and those who eat at his expense. Intelligent men who perpetuate his myth should hang their heads in shame.' Professor Galbraith himself was, of course, a highly enterprising US ambassador, very much in his own right, to Delhi.

The complexity of the activities in foreign countries of the innumerable US agencies is barely credible. In Bonn, for instance, the ambassador ostensibly bears responsibility for thirty-four US agencies, covers highly important relations with top commanders of all fighting services in NATO, and supervises West Berlin affairs. AID is described as 'an autonomous arm of the Department of State', with its own under-secretary of state—a far more powerful official than his opposite number in the Foreign Office. Of AID's 17,000 employees, 14,000 roam the world, trying to develop local resources in anything you care to name from nursing to water supply. The Peace Corps collaborates on similar projects: 30,000 people apply to serve each year. The US foreign aid budget runs at about $1 billion on military support, but excluding emergency military operations as in Vietnam; and some $2 billion on economic and social development. It is not surprising if influential American critics ask whether it is all worth while, diplomatically and in the human results achieved. Then the USIA runs 218 posts in 104 countries, with some 1,300 officers, and pounds out 15,000 hours per week from over 3,000 radio stations abroad. Some 700 million people see their documentaries and newsreels every year. So the communists by no means have the propaganda field to themselves.

In all, the US Foreign Service itself numbers some 11,000 staff. A sample career would begin with five months' training at the Foreign Service Institute in Washington, with courses for wives, followed by four years abroad, then two years at home with perhaps some hard-language training. Six years abroad might follow, some of them possibly with AID or the Peace Corps; then three years in Washington, including perhaps one at the War College. In due course the diplomat might become a member of the policy planning staff; and retire at sixty, unless he has reached the grade of 'career minister' in which case he would stay on until the age of sixty-five. There are about sixty of these: those abroad are almost all ambassadors, while twenty-nine are stationed in the US, of whom ten are in residence at universities.

In February 1970 the Department of State requested, for the fiscal year 1971, a budget of some $450 million, an increase of nearly $50 million. Contributions to international organizations were to total $145 million, an increase of some $15 million. While salaries were put at $22 million, representation allowances totalled a modest $1 million. Senior State Department officers were then quizzed by the sub-committee of the Committee on Appropriations of the House of Representatives on such a scale that the report covered 780 pages. The Secretary of State himself, the Hon. William P. Rogers, was not spared: in his case the discussion lasted two hours, off the record. Nor is that all. Under a procedure lasting several months the State Department's budget has to be finally approved by the Committees on Appropriations of both houses, and to secure final approval by the Senate. An exhaustive, and for some officials exhausting, process. And the Senate's preoccupation with foreign policy by no means ends there. Senators travel far and wide all round the globe observing the Foreign Service's performance; and woe betide the US ambassador or his staff who does not treat them as a cross between royalty and the Secretary of State.

The testing of the State Department and Foreign Service goes much further, however. The tradition of a comparatively small but highly influential body of men inside the White House, with the final vetting responsibility on what is called national security but is very largely foreign policy, is now firmly established. In President Kennedy's day they were headed by Walt Rostow; and Chester Cooper, a member of the group, has shown clearly in *The Lost Crusade* how they, together with a strong Secretary of Defense in Robert McNamara, overruled a weak Secretary of State in the person of Dean Rusk, and egged on first Kennedy and then Johnson to the escalation in Vietnam. (Cooper himself quit when he could no longer influence matters in a sensible direction.) Noam Chomsky roundly condemns for the Vietnam disaster 'The Rusks, McNamaras, Bundys and Rostows', all of them 'considered to be among the ablest, the most humane and liberal men that could be found for public trust', and suggests that they 'should be judged by the principles of Nuremberg if we are to be honest with ourselves'.

Today the *éminence grise*—though no longer, indeed, operating in the shadows—is Dr Henry Kissinger. All the experience, evaluation and wisdom of the State Department has to be filtered through Kissinger and his staff before reaching President Nixon. So far, it must be said in favour of this curious system, the results seem to be looking forward in the direction of *détente* with the communists, rather than backward to any perpetuation of the cold war. But one effect is to drive Mr William Rogers and his staffs in the State Department and the Foreign Service on to the defensive. They are largely relegated to the role of collectors of information, with little influence on policy. Dr Kissinger put it this way in 1969: 'When bureaucracies are so unwieldy and when their internal morale becomes a serious problem, an unpopular decision can be fought by brutal means, such as leaks to the press or congressional committees. Thus, the only way secrecy can be kept is to exclude from the making of the decision all those who are theoretically charged with carrying it out.' This is indeed the new secret diplomacy in action. And Dr Kissinger himself, backed by a personal staff of some 175, combines three roles of the highest importance: presiding over the National Security Council, now the ultimate policy-making body, below the President of course, on foreign affairs and defence; ensuring that the President's orders are carried out; and acting as envoy very extraordinary and supremely plenipotentiary.

Once again, this is far from the end of the complicated story. The mighty Central Intelligence Agency, sometimes described as the 'invisible government', reaches out its tentacles into all the corners of the world covered by the Foreign Service, and a good many odd little corners which the latter cannot properly cover. This is not the place to go into details on the CIA's activities, which I attempt to do in a later chapter on the role of intelligence in diplomacy. But it is appropriate to say here that the Agency constitutes a full second foreign service. Its members are everywhere; in some places more numerous than the career diplomats. They come in all ranks: one or two have been called ambassadors. Their enormous resources enable them to tap information, of course military as well as political and economic, from many sources beyond those open to the diplomats: you could hardly dress USAF Lieutenant Gary Powers up as a diplomatic second secretary and send him over the USSR in a U2. Officially, of course, the CIA's job is to collect information, evaluate it, and pass it on to the local ambassador and the State Department. The reality is different. The local ambassador is often left out of the operation. The CIA's evaluation often leads on to policy-making and action in the field, sometimes large-scale counter-revolutionary action. Where the head of the British Secret Intelligence

Service is a grade two diplomatic official, the head of the CIA, Richard Helms, is a member of the President's inner cabinet, the National Security Council, on a par with the Secretary of State and the Secretary of Defense.

Another powerful influence on American diplomacy is that of the think-tanks. The most prestigious is the RAND Corporation ('Research and No Development'), which is a non profit-making organization and pays no taxes. It was founded in 1946 to 'further and promote scientific, educational and charitable [*sic*] purposes, all for the public welfare and security of the USA'. Put more simply, it was formed by the US Air Force to plan its future strategic systems. One that it planned led to defence measures costing $20 billion which soon proved so inadequate that they had to be supplemented at a cost of a further $15 billion. There are about twenty think-tanks of varying calibre in the US today, employing about 12,000 people. It seems to me quite out of the question that they earn their keep in the realms of defence and foreign policy. We have nothing remotely comparable in Britain and we are none the worse off for that.

Finally, to pile Pelion on Ossa, there is the immense influence on American international relations of the Pentagon and the military–industrial complex, against which President Eisenhower, though himself a general, uttered a firm warning. The Pentagon system has been described—accurately, according to Noam Chomsky—as 'the second largest state management in the world'. Even an official State Department handout says frankly that, 'since World War II, US military commitments and the functions of the military members of the Country Team [i.e. US diplomatic representation in any given country] have mushroomed throughout the free world. In many countries the US has Military Assistance Advisory Groups (MAAG).' It does not draw attention to the fact that the US military involvement in Vietnam, including over 600,000 men at its peak, developed from one of these innocent-sounding Assistance Advisory Groups. Richard J. Barnet covered the scene in *The Economy of Death*, published in 1969; and as he has served in both the Departments of State and of Defense, and was co-director of the independent Institute for Policy Studies in Washington, he was well qualified to do so. He reckons that seventy cents of each budget dollar is spent on 'past, present and future wars'. Statistically the likelihood of nuclear war increases all the time; and the influence of the military has led the US government to pledge to defend forty-two countries, even if it should mean fighting three major wars at once. In McNamara's day as Secretary of Defense the power of the Pentagon swelled to such an extent that the State Department had little, if any, influence on various vital foreign affairs decisions. In some cases the civilian leaders were even readier than the military to adopt warlike postures: President Kennedy was not immune from this tendency. Barnet considers that 'the Department of Defense, having $45 billion a year to spend in the economy, has become the closest thing to a central planning agency in American society. . . . Breaking up the military–industrial complex means drastically downgrading the role of military power in foreign policy. The fact that the Secretary of Defense rather than the Secretary of State issues the annual Posture Statement is a symbol of the militarization of our foreign policy.' It would appear that Barnet's strictures remain broadly justified today.

Such, briefly, is the complex structure of the American diplomatic apparatus. The State Department and the Foreign Service have frankly voiced their self-criticisms and pin-pointed their shortcomings in a 600-page report, known as the Macomber report, prepared by 250 of their members throughout 1970, on *Diplomacy for the 1970s*. They find that for twenty years the State Department has been suffering from 'intellectual atrophy' and pervading conservatism, with individual secretaries of state either unable or unwilling to stimulate the organization. President Kennedy's description of it as 'a bowlful of jelly' is quoted, as is President Nixon's electoral promise in 1968 to house-clean it from top to bottom. Among the report's hundreds of recommendations is an important one to the effect that a special planning group should be created expressly to put forward a reasoned case deliberately against all prevailing policies and thus perform an 'adversary function'. Career officers should be encouraged to take time out for private studies or work in other government departments, while outsiders should be brought in from time to time. Above all, it is necessary 'to devise an explicit list of US interests abroad and to determine their relative importance to the

US. This would be the basis for developing foreign affairs planning and strategy. In all phases, interests and objectives must be matched to resources and capabilities.' These are indeed wise words, though the report does not go on to consider the fearful complexities produced by the multiplicity of US agencies active in the diplomatic field. Not that such multiplicity is always bad: it can be, and often is, creative, thanks to the rivalries it engenders. But with the future, not merely of international relations but of the human race, largely in American hands, we can only hope and pray that the structural problems will be sorted out before it is too late.

THE SOVIET DIPLOMATIC APPARATUS

The future is also largely in the hands of the Soviet government; and in the field of diplomacy they got seriously organized at about the same time as the United States, that is, shortly after the first world war. Between them they were to revolutionize old-world diplomacy and its apparatus; and remarkably slow the old-world powers were to recognize the fact. To this day, indeed, there is no lack of western European diplomats who consider that their Soviet colleagues are mainly thugs and peasants, and many of their American colleagues not quite gentlemen in the style of old Harold Nicolson. (On the latter point, it is only possible to say thank God for it; the West would be in poor shape if such were the case in the 1970s.)

The Soviet diplomatic apparatus is, like the American one, a functional and highly modernized affair which uses all the methods and men at hand to achieve the objects of the USSR and its allies in the world. I speak elsewhere of the intelligence and subversive activities of the Committee for State Security, or KGB, which are comparable with those of the CIA. But Western propagandists have talked themselves into some illusions about the KGB, which has a far wider scope than many believe. Of course there is the official Foreign Ministry in Moscow, with which foreign diplomats deal. But even when its minister is someone as experienced as Gromyko he is no great power in the land. Khrushchev once remarked jocularly that Gromyko would sit on an iceberg for as long as he ordered him to. Similarly, Soviet ambassadors and their staffs act meticulously on orders from above, and take very little initiative on their own. But behind the scenes the KGB has a powerful supervisory function: it is by no means only a combination of DI5 and DI6, but of the FCO and Home Office as well. Candidates for the more overt sides of the KGB sit examinations, like FCO candidates in Britain. A considerable number operate as diplomats abroad, apart from those whose duties frankly constitute espionage. Some are interchangeable. It is as well to bear in mind this aspect of the Soviet diplomatic apparatus. In general, no expense is spared on the traditional appurtenances of diplomacy: embassies and consulates exist all over the world, missions to international organizations abound, staffs are often huge, accommodation and entertainment lavish. Since the USSR no longer seriously aims at taking over the world for communism but rather at continuing competitive co-existence, and since she has big problems of her own within the communist world, the West would be wise to treat her diplomats as what they in fact mostly are: intelligent, highly-trained men and women who can make a considerable contribution to solving the problems of war or peace, in favour of peace. After all, if it comes to one of two possible crunches—both of which God forbid—the USSR and the rest of eastern Europe will be part of what we broadly call 'the West'.

DENMARK

The great majority of states maintain a diplomatic apparatus on a far smaller scale than those so far discussed, so it is worth taking a look at those of two countries typical respectively of the West and of the communist world: Denmark and East Germany.

In Denmark a unified Foreign Service was set up in 1961, some years before we British got around to it. The old predominance of nobles in the Diplomatic Service has been superseded by more democratic selection (though admittedly Denmark's longest-serving diplomat in London, and a very good one, is a royal prince); and pay and allowances make private means no longer necessary. All career officers can hope to become ambassadors, as outside appointments to the top ranks are now the exception. In 1970 the Danish Ministry of Foreign Affairs employed about 1,500 people, some 650 in the Ministry and some 850 in 50-odd embassies and 25 consulates abroad. The senior career officers numbered no more than 280. In addition, attachés specializing in export promotion and information activities are an important part of the apparatus. The Minister of Foreign Affairs supervises all foreign trade matters, as Denmark has never had a ministry of foreign trade, with the help of a minister for European market relations, and another for technical co-operation with developing countries and for disarmament questions. The Foreign Ministry's principal branch handles economic affairs; political and legal affairs come only second. Great emphasis is laid on the importance of assistance to developing countries. The authorities recognize that the Ministry needs reorganizing and restructuring, with particular reference to this last sector of foreign policy. In the interests of economy Denmark appoints various ambassadors to more than one country; and she regards her missions to such international organizations as the UN, NATO, EFTA and the EEC as among her most important. Heads of mission are expressly instructed to show initiative; and the recognized basis of Danish diplomacy is that it, and the Foreign Service which executes it, should and can never be static. In a word, the Danish diplomatic apparatus is inspired by all the right ideas for the 1970s and after.

THE GERMAN DEMOCRATIC REPUBLIC

In describing the diplomatic apparatus of East Germany it is of particular importance to define that country's diplomatic situation in the world, since in the West a good many ideas about it are hazy and a good many others are prejudiced. The standard of living of her citizens is the highest in the communist world. Mainly owing to her own diplomatic efforts, but also thanks to West Germany's Chancellor Willy Brandt's Ostpolitik, East Germany has since 1969 been engaged in establishing diplomatic, and quasi-diplomatic, relations with a rapidly increasing number of nations far and wide. As of 1972 she had full diplomatic relations with thirty-two nations,[1] about half of them non-communist, and the number is constantly increasing. Her inter-state relations, based on an exchange of consulates-general or trade missions, extend to about eighty nations, including Britain.

[1] This number had doubled by January 1973. One newcomer is Spain, where the Communist Party is banned.

The East German government takes the training of its diplomats with the utmost seriousness. The starting point is that the Western tradition that diplomats should come from the gentlemanly class is out; even more so the West German habit of employing, even today, a number of enthusiastic ex-nazis. A high official states: 'The main prerequisite for becoming a diplomat is a firm class standpoint. As we are a workers' and farmers' state most of our diplomats naturally come from the working class. They are educated in the spirit of international understanding and respect for other peoples.' For this purpose aspiring diplomats, selected from those with a good degree in languages or history, a devotion to Marxist–Leninism and a satisfactory record of national military service, are trained for no less than five years at the Institute of International Relations, which is part of the Walter Ulbricht Academy of State and Law Sciences at Babelsberg, near Berlin. Special emphasis is placed on languages, social sciences and economics, with legal studies not far behind. Many of them also go to the Moscow Institute of International Relations, where they can learn not only Russian but such languages as Indonesian, Arabic, Urdu and so on.

The East German diplomat's duties when abroad are defined in terms not so very different from those of the West's representatives. First, he must represent his own country's interests *vis-à-vis* his host country, and for that purpose keep up completely with the developing policies of his own country. Second, he must equally sharply keep his government informed of local developments and tendencies. Third—a little difference here— he must always work to develop 'proletarian internationalism'. Finally, he must protect the interests of his country and her citizens in the host country.

East Germany does not have a foreign branch corresponding to that of the KGB, the CIA or the British SIS as such. Her diplomats are expected not to be too fussy about performing a few extra-curricular duties. (May I add that this is not entirely unknown in some British diplomats' careers. When I was in our legation in Sofia in early 1941, with the nazi army coming in, I agreed to convey two limpet mines across the city in the boot of my car to some reliable Bulgarian agents of ours, who later used them to good effect.) In style and manner the great majority of

East German diplomats are conventional. Their numbers are not excessive. Their activities are not dictated by the Kremlin but, as we have seen, co-ordinated with those of other 'socialist' countries. The diplomacy of East Germany has had, and continues to have, rather special success in the less and least developed countries, particularly in Africa, Asia and Latin America. In those countries of this type where there is also West German representation, the East German representatives are often more acceptable to, and influential with, the local government.

This extends, often enough, to the training of new African or Asian diplomats. Their governments, with their embryonic diplomatic services, tend to turn more for this important facility to the USSR, to East Germany or to China, than to their old colonial masters. This fact is bound to have an increasing influence on the nature of diplomacy as time goes on.

CHAPTER NINE

The Role of Intelligence

Many of my best friends are spies. That is to say, naturally, that they are loyal members of the British Secret Intelligence Service and of the American Central Intelligence Agency. It is true that I have also known in the past spies of a different type; the traitors Maclean, Burgess and Philby, as they happened to be my contemporaries. But that is another story. As diplomacy's first and foremost object is to gain accurate and full information about other countries or organizations, and then to assess it correctly in the light of all the relevant factors so that a sensible decision can be reached on policy, it is clear that the role of intelligence is a considerable one.

Many members of the public are interested in the workings and significance of intelligence, and feel frustrated by the extent to which they are kept in ignorance. It is obvious that secret intelligence has to be kept secret; but it is also true that the antiquated Official Secrets Acts, of which I have more to say elsewhere, are on occasion used merely to conceal facts or actions which are embarrassing or inconvenient to those in power, without being dangerous secrets at all.

The reason that I know 'the friends', as they are technically described in the business, is that I was a member of the intelligence community for some years, although a career diplomat, and ended that particular—and particularly enjoyable—stint as the Foreign Office adviser to the chief of the secret service, or 'C' for short. Since a good many misconceptions are published about the intelligence machine, sometimes by politicians and journalists who should know better, it may be appropriate here to give the facts.

The SIS, also known as the Secret Service, DI (for Defence Intelligence) 6, 'a branch of the FCO', or in the past as MI (for Military Intelligence) 6, is responsible for collecting intelligence from abroad. In passing, not one of my friends is at all similar to James Bond, or cares whether his or her dry martini is shaken or stirred. Their job is to collect and evaluate intelligence, either off their own bat or through agents, genially known as 'joes', whom they control, or again through electronic and other devices. Their head man, 'C', is therefore the equivalent of Ian Fleming's 'M'. The internal organization of the SIS, as might be expected, roughly parallels that of the FCO, with separate regional, functional, and administrative departments. The SIS works alongside the Security Services, or DI5, an entirely separate organization devoted to counter-intelligence whose head is the director-general, or DGSS. Co-operation is usually, but not invariably, close.

These two services have representatives on the co-ordinating intelligence body, the Defence Intelligence Committee. This appellation has replaced the long-established title of Joint Intelligence Committee; and I regret this because the military connotation appears to have superseded the more general one. However, the important thing is that the DIC is still, like the JIC in the past, usually chaired by a very senior FCO member rather than by a military person. It includes representatives of the armed services and co-opts as necessary experts, such as scientists, kremlinologists, and sinologists, when the matters in hand appear to warrant it. The DIC's duty is to supply responsible ministers and officials with up-to-the-minute intelligence on critical matters, forecasts of trouble or other significant developments, and longer-term round-ups. Their sphere of action extends far beyond that of defence in the narrow sense, to include political and economic matters and so on: in fact all matters of potential interest to the government, and particularly to the FCO and the Department of Defence. Co-operation between the British and US secret and security services is close both in London and Washington and, to a greater or lesser degree, depending on varying local interests, in other countries round the world.

The FCO has three departments in direct liaison with the DIC: the defence policy, the defence training and supply and the Permanent Under-Secretary's departments. (I was for a time head of the last-named, and chairman of the Deputy Directors' JIC.) There is, or should be, constant interaction between the FCO and the sis, the former normally putting forward their requirements and the latter thinking up means of meeting them. These means should again have the broad approval of the fco as regards their political implications, though obviously details are left to the experts of the sis. Alternatively, the sis can come up with their own bright ideas for approval. But it would be considered naughty of them to indulge in too much private enterprise of their own. On occasion there can be a slip-up in the procedure and execution, as there was when poor Commander Crabb greeted Bulganin and Khrushchev in 1956 by swimming about under their cruiser in Portsmouth harbour.

The British and the Russians have practised secret intelligence gathering for centuries, though in the United States it was regarded as not gentlemanly until the Japanese showed at Pearl Harbor that this attitude could put you at a serious disadvantage in a world which was full of non-gentlemen. Pearl Harbor constituted all the more extreme a case as the us communications technicians, a highly able body of men, had cracked many of the Japanese codes and reported to the us government that something sinister was in the offing. With typical American energy a makeshift, but very active, service called the Office of Strategic Services was set up, in close consultation with the British sis. In 1947 the Central Intelligence Agency was formed with the help of Kim Philby, who must have derived much malicious pleasure in the process.

That baby rapidly grew into a powerful giant, now housed in a vast complex of offices in Langley, Virginia. Congressional testimony released in May 1970 indicated that the us military intelligence agencies, of which there are four, alone employed over 136,000 people and spent almost $3,000 million a year. This was apart from the intelligence activities of the cia, the State Department and a couple of other agencies. When the Assistant Secretary of Defense for Administration was asked to guess the total annual intelligence bill he declined, but with masterly understatement agreed that 'it is considerable' and even 'frightening'. Educated guesses in fact put it at between $5,000 million and $6,000 million, or something like the entire British defence budget. The total number of people employed, world-wide, may well be some 300,000. In spite of all this effort us intelligence has spectacularly failed to satisfy President Nixon on Vietnam affairs;[1] and, to the chagrin of Congress, he has brought its operations more under the control of the ubiquitous Dr Kissinger, who already wields power in so many fields.

The British SIS admits publicly to expenditure of just over £10 million a year; this is of course a notional figure and the real costs are undoubtedly higher, though still infinitesimal compared with those of the CIA or the Soviet Committee of State Security (Komitet Gosudarstvennoi Bezopastnosti). The KGB is not in the habit of publishing its expenditure, but its activities cover the world in much the same way as those of the CIA. In some directions their operations are less lavishly executed than the CIA's, but as they are comparable in extent and intensity the USSR clearly devotes a greater proportion of its GNP to them than does the US.

The existence and active functioning of these two mammoth apparatuses is as striking a manifestation as any of the depth of mistrust and the extreme tension existing between the superpowers ever since the second world war. The two governments both consider the huge expenditure of money and manpower necessary to their security and diplomacy.

But are they really necessary in fact? I should say certainly not on their present scale. When I was Foreign Office adviser to the chief of the SIS, then Sir Dick White, I shocked some of my intelligence colleagues by saying that there could be such a thing as too much intelligence on any given matter. The CIA is certainly prone to this exaggeration in the political sphere. What is apt to happen is that masses of information pours in from different sources, some of them perhaps professional pedlars. Much will be repetitive, which clogs the machine for a start. But equally, on some points it will differ, to a more or less subtle extent. Here the difficulty of assessment and interpretation sets in. The best intelligence officers are perfectly honest men; but they are human, and if one among several possible assessments falls into line with some desirable policy or plan of action, it is natural enough that it may be adopted. The CIA is organized in four divisions: intelligence, plans, research and support. The danger points are plans and support. For the CIA has long since abandoned the

[1] He recently dismissed its head, Richard Helms.

traditional SIS idea that intelligence must be 'pure', or in other words that on no account must one and the same organization both assess the intelligence and base policy and action on it. A long list of major CIA 'special operations', entailing the overthrow of foreign governments considered hostile to US interests, ranges from Iran and Guatemala in the 1950s to Cambodia in 1970. The general tendency of these operations has always been, and continues to be, hawkishly anti-communist and even sometimes anti-neutralist. The KGB is organized on similar lines and is equipped to undertake similar operations in the opposite direction. In practice these operations have recently been less far-flung and aggressive than those of the CIA. For sheer ruthlessness the two bodies are on a par. And, ironically enough, there have been occasions of extreme tension when the two bitterly opposed organizations have collaborated, in the utmost secrecy of course, to prevent the situation from getting totally out of hand.

But, as in other branches of diplomacy, the top targets are not just political or diplomatic. In our age the safety, and the very life, of the US and the USSR, and perhaps of humanity as a whole, depends on the super-powers having accurate and early intelligence on the thermo-nuclear capabilities and potentialities which each possesses at any given moment. That being the case, almost any expenditure of money and manpower might seem justifiable. The methods vary through the whole range from very large to very small. The spy satellites circling the world are now an accepted part of the system. They report with formidable accuracy on even the tiniest targets. But equally, an indiscreet remark by, say, a nuclear physicist on either side when in his cups could provide a lead to some dangerous new development. The revelations of a well-placed defector can be as valuable as the best efforts of a sophisticated machine. He may be able to throw light not only on the organization of some intelligence or military body but positively on its policy for the future. It is equally important to know, for instance, not just the location of a possible enemy's ICBMs, but the moment when he intends to use them: this is where 'humint', as the Americans call it, forms an essential part of the picture. George Blake, for instance, was of inestimable use to the KGB for a variety of reasons. He could, and did, betray and disrupt a major Anglo-American undertaking such as the Berlin tunnel. He could keep the KGB up to date on Anglo-American intelligence and diplomatic policy and intentions. He could send them a regular round-up of the deployment of our agents, and for that matter of our clandestine operations, in many parts of the world. It was not for nothing that the Lord Chief Justice of England pronounced sweepingly that 'he rendered most of Britain's efforts completely useless'. Not, you see, just Britain's intelligence efforts. Lord Chief Justice Parker had in mind our efforts in the sphere of international relations generally, of diplomacy.

As in other spheres of British diplomacy, so in the crypto-diplomatic sphere it has to be asked: do we need the SIS, and is it worth while? I think that the answer too is similar: yes, but with limited objectives and responsibilities. The SIS has never been large in numbers, nor has it spent large sums of money. Unlike the CIA and the KGB it has never had one of its own professionals as its chief. Up till the present the chief has always been a retired general or admiral, with one exception: Sir Dick White, who before then had been a lifelong professional in what was then MI5, the Security Services. Today the chief is a career diplomat, Sir John Ogilvy Rennie,[1] a deputy under-secretary or grade two official. This can only be an inhibiting and restraining influence, turning the SIS into a sort of second-class diplomatic service, whereas previous chiefs were in a position to pick up the telephone and speak direct to the Prime Minister or one of his Cabinet colleagues. Not that we want a huge independent body like the CIA. The chain of command in head office has always gone up through the ranks of the SIS via the Foreign and Commonwealth Office adviser, who will consult FCO departments as necessary, to C, who with the agreement of his adviser will submit his plans and ideas to the deputy under-secretary responsible for all intelligence and strategic matters in the FCO. He in turn can either approve the project, or consult yet higher authority in the shape of the Permanent Under-Secretary or the Secretary of State. C also has the right to submit urgent raw intelligence direct to ministers, while keeping the FCO informed; but wherever possible it is preferable that it should be collated and assessed first, as ministers are prone to jumping to wrong conclusions if

[1] He is to retire in 1973.

they are not presented with the picture as a whole. There is also talk of a professional diplomat taking over supreme command of all our intelligence and security services.[1]

The higher ranks of the SIS are almost all upper class, just as those of the CIA are mainly Ivy League. I am not sure that this matters: the best of them are capable of imaginative planning, and of setting in motion dirty work without soiling their own hands. In any case the identity of almost all of the senior members of the service is known to the KGB. By the time they have achieved seniority in the Service their duties consist of planning operations and compiling responsible assessments, and maintaining liaison with friendly intelligence services, while the agents and devices in the field look after the provision of raw intelligence.

A good deal of ingenuity goes into providing cover for senior spooks serving abroad; not always with great success, for the same reasons as those affecting their similar ranking colleagues at head office. Often, too, they are in quite close liaison with the local intelligence services, and to some extent the question of cover may be of only secondary importance. Fairly frequent use is made of businessmen or others having close connections with a foreign country, sometimes on a once-for-all basis. Poor Greville Wynne discovered that such activities can have dire results. A far greater proportion of the CIA's staff and operations is overt; though one American journalist complained recently that 'It is a secret now if a third-rate bureaucrat blows his nose'. When abroad, members of the SIS are under orders to be especially circumspect on all clandestine work that might affect diplomatic relations with the country where they reside or with its close allies. But they naturally have direct contact with their head office in London; and they would be saints, rather than human beings, if in the occasional burst of inspiration, or of exasperation with the official diplomats, they did not deploy a little private enterprise. The traditional British ambassador used to regard all this activity as ungentlemanly and a waste of time and money. But the traditional British ambassador is, happily, fading into a well-merited oblivion. Most of our heads of mission today, and their younger colleagues who will be the ambassadors of tomorrow, have a proper respect for the activities of

[1] Sir Peter Wilkinson's appointment was announced in January 1973.

the SIS, so long as they are kept reasonably well-informed—and the enterprises yield results.

With the CIA and the KGB the position is quite different. One official US report on the position of CIA and military representatives in embassies ventured the judgement that 'to a degree the primacy of the ambassador is a polite fiction'. It is not unknown for the CIA to provide the ambassador himself from its ranks, though this is rare; and its degree of independence is indicated by the publicly-made accusation that, together with the other powerful US intelligence agencies, it constitutes an 'invisible government' of the US. The head of the CIA, for a long time Allen Dulles, brother of Secretary of State John Foster Dulles— a power-wielding family, that one—and now Richard Helms, has the legal right to spend hundreds of millions of dollars annually on his own say-so and without any accountability to the US government. He is ex-officio a member of the President's inner cabinet. It is hardly surprising that the CIA takes a strong hand in some policy decisions, though Allen Dulles tried in a rather embarrassed way to maintain that it stopped short of this. The KGB has further powers again. It is accepted that it has responsibilities for the USSR's international relations on a par with those of the Soviet External Affairs Department, both answering only to the Politburo of the Communist Party of the Soviet Union. Their cover stratagems for members of their service abroad are far more flexible than those of other intelligence services: their head representative in an embassy may literally be anyone from the ambassador to his chauffeur or chef.

I think that our little SIS can still do useful work in a limited sphere, though it would be better placed with a professional at its head, still reporting of course to the head of the FCO. Where nuclear matters are concerned it can only keep its eyes and ears open in the hope of picking up something that might just add a little to the intelligence procured by our allies. In the economic sphere it can keep generally alert, and not least collate intelligence collected from overt sources, whether human or written. But as its main aim it should concentrate on a few good operations to bring across defectors well placed to communicate information, from as near the centre as possible, on the intentions and policy of potential opponents in all these spheres. And in all these spheres it should collaborate closely with DI5. Britain's desperate need, after all, is peace; and though in the past DI6 has tended to look down on DI5 as a service devoted to the shuffling about of card indexes, the latter's value has for many years been considerable and is better appreciated today. Like DI6, DI5 is subject to higher authority, in this case in both the FCO and the Home Office. Some of its clandestine operations, though by definition of the organization's responsibilities they are carried out on home ground, are also capable of making a considerable contribution to our diplomatic policy and operations. Incidentally, intelligence services of all countries are sometimes unfairly accused of failing in not foretelling some unfavourable development, when the fact is that the originators of that development had not made up their own minds to action until the last moment —in other words where the development and timing were literally unpredictable. In passing, I think there was no excuse for our complete lack of intelligence in the West, Berlin then being an undivided city, on the communists' intention to erect that cumbrous wall in the night of 12 to 13 August 1961, in spite of our plethora of agents and the complicated logistics on the communist side of getting all the materials into position. But our intelligence morale, as I have already suggested, had been shattered as a result of George Blake's activities.

Mention should be made of the Government Communications Headquarters (GCHQ), which works near staid Cheltenham. Here the staff consists largely of boffins, mathematicians and first-class chess players. It is described as a department of the FCO engaged in research, development and production of communications equipment. In these days rapid and secure communications are of more importance than ever in the conduct of international relations, both to any given country, such as ours, and to its possible opponents. The KGB has a powerful section devoted to this kind of work, and makes no bones about it extending to the making and breaking of codes and cyphers. The same goes for the huge US National Security Agency, rightly respected for its expertise in this direction. According to a recent report its budget is some £400 million a year, and it employs about 100,000, mainly military personnel.

However, this book is about diplomacy and not about intelligence as such. James Bond lives again, and the cloak and the dagger flourish, to some extent, in the jumbo services of the CIA and the KGB. The SIS is more pedestrian, but if efficiently run it can form a modest, though still useful, part of our diplomatic apparatus. It can obtain intelligence on secret matters and pass it on to the policy-makers. It can maintain contacts with people and organizations that our above-board diplomats, and even businessmen, cannot conveniently tackle—like the anti-diplomats of Algiers, for instance. Thus it can sometimes give warning of intended action by opposition groups that may change the whole political atmosphere in a country, though the reporting of random semi-secret political tittle-tattle is of little importance. It can keep going a two-way traffic with the mighty CIA, to the advantage, if unequal, of both. In view of the past record it must watch itself carefully for the presence of traitors; not that the US or the Soviet intelligence services have a clean bill in this respect. And if the SIS's position, together with that of Britain in the world, will never empower us to remove unfriendly governments in foreign countries, it will never lead to a Bay of Pigs, a Vietnam or a Czechoslovakia either.

CHAPTER TEN

The Diplomatic Corps

For most people in the world diplomacy is both a portentous and a puzzling word. Portentous, because of all the trappings. In every capital the leading ambassadors inhabit the best and most grandiose houses; in the major capitals veritable palaces, such as the British embassy building in Paris or that of the US embassy in London. The ceremonial attached to the presentation of an ambassador's letters of credence to the head of the host state is elaborate. In London the Sovereign's coach and horses convey the ambassador, either festooned with gold braid, plumed hat and sword, or wearing full evening dress and white tie or gorgeous tribal robes, to Buckingham Palace at eleven in the morning, disrupting the normal traffic in the process. In Moscow the ceremonial is no less solemn, though not as anachronistic in execution. *Punch* devoted a number to the question: 'Are diplomats necessary?' The pictorial front page depicts ambassadors in London, in full fig, proceeding to present their credentials, with the comment: 'If you asked me who needs them, I'd say without a moment's hesitation: Moss Bros.' One article is devoted to: 'A necessary luxury. A defence of diplomatic uselessness'.

Everywhere diplomats appear to ordinary people to be obsessed with the pomposities of protocol and precedence. It is true that rather too much time is wasted on such matters even today; but it is also the case that they can serve a useful purpose in, for instance, preventing petty disputes between diplomats from widely differing national backgrounds. Protocol should be the oil which keeps the diplomatic machinery functioning sweetly, rather than living a life of its own. Then it is well known that diplomats indulge in a constant round of parties, from formal luncheons and dinners to semi-formal cocktails and even working breakfasts. 'Jennifer's Diary' would be a poor thing without all those diplomatic junketings. One elderly ambassador friend of mine complained that the endless round of cocktail parties had caused his arches to collapse, and described such parties as 'the scourge of the century'. Best of all, when the socialist President Nasser visited the socialist Soviet Union, he was entertained to a 'banquet'; and so was President Nixon in communist Peking. Lord Trevelyan has some typically shrewd and dry remarks on this question in his book *Worlds Apart*. 'As Malcolm Muggeridge reported from Moscow, diplomats and cows eat standing. Several times a week the same faces gathered round the table at an embassy or at the Praga Restaurant for somebody's national day. If you cut a new embassy's national day without good excuse, you offended your host, and the Russians, who were there in force, scored a point. The endless round of these functions was no great hardship and gave opportunities for contacts which would otherwise have been difficult to obtain, though after two years it all became a bit stale.' He also relates how at one of these celebrations Mr Attlee slept peacefully through an hour's speechifying, while he himself had the daydream of inflicting on a diplomatic audience a speech of ten hours about the liberation of England from the Danes.

DIPLOMATIC PRIVILEGES

So much for the portentous side. There is much that is puzzling, too. Can one and the same sort of 'envoy', to use the journalistic blanket term, be fairly asked at one post to discuss matters of crucial world importance such as SALT and to cope with rescuing the British football captain Bobby Moore from a charge trumped up by some Colombians in Bogotá?

Then there is the tremendous proliferation of diplomats. In London, for instance, the diplomatic corps consists of hundreds of people representing some 120 countries and organizations. All who qualify for inclusion in the diplomatic list are completely immune from British law; they could literally get away with murder. Major offences are of course very rare, but the number of parking offences by foreign diplomats is legion; and I myself had the experience of a Latin American envoy refusing to pay some bills in connection with my house which I had rented to him, with the support of his ambassador for his refusal. What is more, all diplomats are taken on trust, so to speak, by the host country: it is the diplomat's own government that decides he is to appear on the list. Thus even a medium-sized embassy will boast an ambassador, a minister, a counsellor or two, a couple of service attachés, various first, second, and third secretaries, plus attachés. If any of these misbehaves in London the only action that the British authorities can take is to request the head of mission to waive the diplomatic privileges of the offending diplomat; or in extreme cases involving, for example, espionage, to declare him *persona non grata*, in other words no longer welcome in the country, and thus get him out. It is indeed open to the host government to decline a head of mission when he or she is proposed, but this of course tends to embitter relations. I have known one or two cases where diplomats could not proceed as intended because their names meant something too ribald in the host country. The senior staff in the 120-odd missions in London vary in number between about eighty in the case of the Soviet embassy to nil in the case of Rwanda, which has an accredited embassy in London but prefers to keep its staff in Brussels. They of course enjoy full privileges when they choose to come here. At present just two heads of mission are women.

This is only the tip of the iceberg. If the total of senior diplomats is to be counted in hundreds, the total of junior officials—from clerks to cooks and chauffeurs—attached to missions in London reaches thousands; and though they do not enjoy full diplomatic privileges they have various advantages denied to the British citizen. This annoys some of those citizens, not surprisingly, and critical questions are fairly often asked in Parliament.

The situation is of course similar in Washington, New York or Paris. In theory the basis of the arrangement is reciprocity; but in practice it is in many cases impossible to achieve this completely. In all communist countries, for instance, foreign diplomats tend to be regarded as spies, because the communist governments assume that they will be given the same assignments as a considerable proportion of their own representatives. Consequently the communist authorities keep a very sharp eye on them and often hamper their movements; we can reciprocate either by taking similar measures, which consume much time and manpower since hundreds of diplomats are involved, or by just hoping for the best. In practice our attitude is the usual one of British compromise: we watch and we hamper in some special cases, but not in all. Again, some might say that total reciprocity, at least of amenities, was not achieved between the diplomat from Ouagadougou posted to London and the gentleman sent there from Whitehall. But in diplomacy you have to take the rough with the smooth. The distinguished American diplomat Charles Thayer puts it this way:

> Coddled and pampered behind this formidable barrier of international law and custom, untouchable by the police, beyond the reach of the tax collector and the customs inspector, the diplomatic corps, one might suppose, would be the world's greatest breeding ground for adult delinquents. However, along with the immunities there has developed a diplomatic ethic based largely on custom which more or less adequately takes the place of the laws from which diplomats are exempt.

George Gale of *The Spectator* is less kindly. Referring to the numerous abductions of diplomats he comments that, not being one himself, he regards it as 'a civilized practice, and certainly very sensible. . . . There are too many diplomats anyway, all with their quite unnecessary privileges.' He confesses, however, that many people will not share his views. He also refers to our successful ambassador John Freeman as 'that rat-trap collectivist'. He goes on to applaud the appointment of the unequivocally right-wing Earl of Cromer, who did not particularly distinguish himself when he was financial minister in Washington, as ambassador there in these terms: 'The aristocracy is better suited for diplomacy; it is trained to the theatrical part of life. An ambassador is not only an agent, he is a spectacle.' It is people and opinions such as these that gravely hinder the effectiveness of our diplomacy in the 1970s.

If the diplomatic apparatus is no longer the glittering affair of balls, sumptuous uniforms and arcane discussions that it once was, it is nevertheless considered essential by every independent state, however great or small. No sooner was the conclusion of the negotiations for the independence of Cyprus in sight than Archbishop Makarios sent the secretary-general designate of the future Foreign Ministry along to me to get my advice on how to set up the apparatus. Recently the Republic of Maldives celebrated its new-found independence by establishing diplomatic relations with East Germany: useful to the Germans for spreading the communist doctrine, but presumably a sheer prestige gesture by Maldives. Another prestige gesture was the expenditure by Czechoslovakia, not one of the most prosperous states, of over £1 million on a new embassy in London in 1969. And in the prestige field, it is a fact that in Britain foreign ambassadors are in the thirteenth place after the Queen in the national order of precedence, all 100-plus of them; while ministers plenipotentiary come fifteenth, immediately below dukes. There appears to be plenty of life in the old corps yet.

CHAPTER ELEVEN

The International Organizations

A list of the major bodies is given in appendix 2. As I have already remarked, they come in two principal forms: bodies for discussion, whether of all subjects generally or of certain specific objects, and defence alliances.

THE UNITED NATIONS

The outstanding example of the former type is of course the United Nations, together with its numerous specialized off-shoots. It followed the unsuccessful League of Nations established in 1920; the 'original members' of the UN signed a declaration of intent to set it up in 1942 in Washington. The basis of its charter was laid at a conference of foreign ministers in Moscow in 1943. In June 1945 fifty nations of the anti-nazi alliance put their signatures to the charter in San Francisco, and the UNO formally came into existence on 24 October 1945. Its avowed purposes are to maintain international peace and security by achieving co-operation between nations in every sphere—political, economic, social, cultural, humanitarian—except that of war. Its first principle is the sovereign equality of all its members. The charter begins by enunciating these purposes and principles in detail, and goes on in a further eighteen chapters to deal with such subjects as membership, which is open to all 'peace-loving' nations and subject to the approval of the General Assembly on the recommendation of the Security Council; the General Assembly and the Security Council themselves; action with respect to threats to the peace; the Economic and Social Council; the Trusteeship Council; the International Court of Justice; and the Secretariat. The official and working languages are Chinese, English, French, Russian and Spanish.

The General Assembly consists of all members of the UN, amounting to some 130 at present and possibly some 150 by the time all colonies have been given independence and such anomalies as the exclusion of the divided countries—Germany, Korea, Vietnam—have been put right. The General Assembly can, and does in practice, discuss all matters affecting international relations, and makes recommendations for action to the Security Council. In the Assembly the rule is one nation one vote, though in practice the USSR has four, since the Byelorussian and Ukrainian SSRs have 'independent' votes of their own and Mongolia, although we have a British embassy in Ulan Bator as if it were independent, never votes against the USSR. It has nine main committees, dealing with everything from political and security matters to administrative and budgetary questions. On major issues, including the election of non-permanent members of the Security Council, the affirmative vote of two-thirds of the members present is required, in place of the normal simple majority.

The Security Council, initially eleven strong and now fifteen, has five permanent members: France, the USSR, Britain, the United States and now China. The ten others are elected for two years each, non-prolongable. It bears the primary responsibility for the maintenance of peace and security, including the raising of 'peace forces' such as that in Cyprus. The five permanent members hold the power of veto except on procedural matters. When, in 1972, the Security Council for the first time met outside New York, to be exact in Addis Ababa, there was much criticism of the unnecessary expense and discomfort involved. The expense was in fact negligible compared with that of many of its highly wasteful routine procedures. The discomfort was no more than diplomats should be prepared to face in a good cause, particularly as the Ethiopians are admirable hosts. And the cause proved good indeed, as the meeting gave a great boost to African morale, not least when Britain was forced to use the veto over a resolution strongly condemning our policy towards Smith's Rhodesia. This use of the veto was highly regrettable: one sphere of great importance in which Britain could and should give a lead in the years to come is that of combating every type of racialism. As for the Security Council, I would hope that before long it will hold a meeting in Asia: perhaps in Peking?

Britain's most effective representative at the UN was Lord Caradon, a Privy Councillor and Minister of State at the FCO. He, and the Labour government he represented from 1964 to 1970, took the organization seriously; and thanks to his personal status he had direct access to the Prime Minister and to the Foreign and Commonwealth Secretary. It would be a good thing to revive an appointment on these lines. Today, as before Lord Caradon, we have a grade one ambassador from the Diplomatic Service, worthy indeed but lacking the same pulling weight. His senior staff numbers twenty-six, which is not excessive.

The Economic and Social Council consists of twenty-seven members elected annually by the General Assembly, and meets once a year in New York and once in Geneva. It has four regional economic commissions, in Geneva, Bangkok, Santiago and Addis Ababa. The more important and effective specialized agencies of the UN include the International Atomic Energy Agency with headquarters in Vienna; the International Labour Organization, though this was founded in 1919; the Organization for Food and Agriculture; and on the financial side the International Bank for Reconstruction and Development, the International Finance Corporation, the International Development Association, the International Monetary Fund and the organization of the General Agreement on Tariffs and Trade. All told there are a further eighteen subsidiary organizations and *ad hoc* committees of the General Assembly, including not least the Disarmament Committee. The senior members of the Secretariat are the secretary-general and eleven under-secretaries-general, all of different nationalities. The secretaries-general have been, in turn, Trygve Lie of Norway, Dag Hammarskjöld of Sweden, U Thant of Burma, and now Kurt Waldheim of Austria. For 1972 the UN gross budget appropriation amounted to some $213 million. The UK contributed something over $6\frac{1}{2}$ per cent of this, compared with $31\frac{1}{2}$ per cent from the US, $14\frac{1}{2}$ per cent from the USSR, France's 6 per cent and Japan's $3\frac{3}{4}$ per cent. When the General Assembly approved this record sum the USSR voted against it, and the UK, France and the US abstained. They had all previously appealed for economy and realism.

And what of the UN's performance in practice? It is easy to be critical and facetious. The list of its impeccable purposes and principles was drawn up in the heady days of the grand anti-nazi and anti-fascist alliance. But already by 1944 Stalin was suspicious that his Western allies were not pulling their full weight in the war; and his spies were informing him of the US development of the nuclear weapon, which could possibly be used to destroy all the advantages gained by the USSR at such terrible cost. The story of how the Soviet Union clamped down the Iron Curtain while it worked out its own nuclear deterrent is a familiar one. But who can deny that, perhaps in a rough and ready manner, the UN played an essential part in holding the ring during the most dangerous years of the cold war? Korea, Suez, Cyprus, even Vietnam, bear witness to this. Of course the superpowers and the major powers between them have the last word. But even the smallest powers have a constant opportunity of uttering many of the words, and ideas, before that stage is reached. If they are no doubt often manipulated by the stronger powers, they none the less have a highly organized forum where they can and do have their say. The day could well come when the representative of the Republic of Maldives, for instance, is president of the General Assembly, or a member of the Security Council. Surely this is all to the good. And as my list of dependent bodies has shown, the UN organization as a whole operates in spheres far beyond those of war and peace; in fact in numerous spheres of much greater day-to-day interest to the majority of mankind, including health and the environment, than those terminal matters. Indeed, according to a report by a body called the Joint Inspection Union on Documentation, it is trying too hard and 'is drowning in its own words and suffocating in its own documentation . . . If the trend continues the number of pages to be digested by delegations will have risen from 650 a day in 1970 to 750 in 1980. From being unmanageable the situation will have reached the point of absurdity.' The cost of writing and printing in 1969 was some £15 million. When China formally took her place in the General Assembly in November 1971 there were no fewer than fifty-six welcoming addresses, spinning out for nearly six hours.

It would be idle to pretend that the UN is particularly successful overall. A good deal of comment over the last two or three years has been to the effect that its influence is in decline, and I think that there is some justification for this. In the case of the latest India–Pakistan war it was easily held at arm's length by India until she had completed her victory; and the UN's part in helping the wretched people of Bangladesh after the war continues to be negligible. Another example of failure was the 1972 meeting in Santiago de Chile of the United Nations Committee for Trade and Development (UNCTAD), constituted with the admirable object of narrowing the gap in the standards of living between the affluent and the less developed countries. The upshot here was that the ninety-six representatives of the latter came away disillusioned with the insincerity of the twenty of the former. Nor does China's new membership give much hope for the UN's increased effectiveness. She will merely pursue there her balance of power tactics between the US and the USSR; she will seize every opportunity, in particular, of opposing initiatives by the USSR; and she will exploit all the opportunities offered by close contact in New York to expand her influence in the third and fourth worlds.

In spite of all this, I still believe that it is better, from numerous points of view, to have the UN in existence rather than to lapse into the chaos and lack of communication that would preponderate if it were not there. Consequently, I also believe that we British could find a truly useful new role in supporting it more whole-heartedly than we often have done in the past.

OTHER MULTILATERAL ORGANIZATIONS

Outside the United Nations there are about twenty international organizations of importance, some falling into the consultative category and others into that of defensive alliances; while some come marginally between the two. Among the first category the most worthy of note are the Bank of International Settlements, the Commonwealth, the Council for Mutual Economic Aid (COMECON), the Council of Europe, the European Communities (otherwise the EEC or Common Market), the European Free Trade Area, the Organization for Economic Co-operation and Development, the Organization of African Unity and the Organization of American States. In the marginal category come three bodies of a mainly consultative nature but with defence commitments of a shadowy kind: the Arab League, the Central

Treaty Organization (CENTO) and the South-East Asia Treaty Organization. Finally there are the defence organizations with real teeth: NATO, ANZUS (the security treaty between Australia, New Zealand and the US) and the Warsaw Pact. The teeth are powerful, of course, chiefly because either the US or the USSR is involved in each case.

Obviously the two most influential of these bodies in our thermo-nuclear age are NATO and the Warsaw Pact; much more influential, alas, should it come to the crunch, than the United Nations itself. I express elsewhere in this book my confidence that it will not come to that crunch, my reasons for thinking that it will not and my hopes that, on the contrary, the two alliances can be instrumental in negotiating a *détente* of great significance. Next in importance for our diplomacy comes the question of our entry into the Common Market; and after that the preservation of our links with the Commonwealth and EFTA. It should then be possible to get on terms, in parallel with the NATO–Warsaw Pact ploy, with COMECON.

NATO AND THE WARSAW PACT

Although the history and the nature of these principal bodies are pretty well known, it would seem appropriate to describe them briefly here. NATO was formed in 1949, its members being Belgium, Canada, Denmark, France, Iceland, Italy, Luxembourg, Netherlands, Norway, Portugal, Britain and the US. Greece and Turkey joined in 1952, and West Germany in 1955. In recent years France has half-withdrawn, and Iceland now shows signs of doing the same. NATO leans heavily on the purposes and principles of the UN; but particularly on article 51 of the charter, which emphasizes the members' rights of individual and collective self-defence. It also stresses the democratic character of the organization, which seems problematical since the alliance includes Portugal, Greece and Turkey, with Spain lending close support from outside. To put it plainly, the treaty had three main objectives: to stop communist expansion in Europe; to keep US forces engaged there; and to re-arm West Germany in the Western camp under suitable safeguards. The top authority, the North Atlantic Council, meets at ministerial level twice or more a year. The permanent representatives of all the allies, headed by ambassadors, meet at least once a week in the headquarters in Brussels. Ours is a grade one ambassador, with a senior staff of fifteen. The Supreme Allied Commander has always been a US general; the UK of course contributes some of his deputies in all three services, and many thousands of men to boot. Britain's financial contribution to the NATO secretariat is some £1¼ million, and to NATO military agencies some £8½ million.

The Warsaw Pact was the tit-for-tat from the communist side. Signed in 1955, when West Germany joined NATO, its signatories were Albania (who has since withdrawn), Bulgaria, Czechoslovakia, Hungary, East Germany, Poland, Romania and the USSR. The treaty's expressed main purpose is to create a system of collective security in Europe founded on the participation of all European states irrespective of their social and political character. Like NATO, it leans heavily on the principles and objectives of the UN. It also observes that a dangerous military grouping has been set up, in the shape of NATO. Like NATO again, the Pact has a high-powered political consultative committee, and a unified command of the armed forces, in practice always with a Soviet supremo.

THE VARIOUS EUROPEAN COMMUNITIES

Until 1973 the European Communities comprised Benelux, France, West Germany and Italy, with Greece and Turkey associated and aiming at eventual membership; Britain, the Republic of Ireland and Denmark became members of 1 January 1973. The treaty of Paris of 1952 established the first body, the European Coal and Steel Community; and the treaties of Rome of 1957 the European Economic Community, or Common Market and the European Atomic Energy Community. A single Commission of the Communities came into being in July 1967; but a single European Community awaits a new treaty to replace those of Paris and Rome. The European Commission, whose duty is to initiate policy, consists of nine members, two each nominated by West Germany, France, Italy (and prospectively Britain) and one each by the other members. Above the Commission comes the Council of Ministers nominated by each of the member states, which takes decisions on the Commission's proposals. The European Parliament, of 142 members elected by the legislatures of the member states, has the right of consultation and discussion, and also of dismissing the Commission. Finally, the Court of Justice has seven members and is the supreme court in all matters relating to the Communities. The Yaoundé Convention of 1964 established a special relationship with eighteen formerly dependent African territories. Need I say more to show what a super-power the Communities could become if, with their prospective new recruits, they direct their policies in a dynamic global direction, and avoid the temptation of becoming a self-centred rich man's club.[1]

As for EFTA, this far less ambitious association was formed under the Stockholm Convention in 1960, signed by Austria, Denmark, Norway, Portugal, Sweden, Switzerland and the UK; with Finland becoming an associate member in 1961 and Iceland a full member in 1970. It has done good by progressively eliminating restrictions on trade between the member states, but it is of course in no way designed to rival the achievements and potential of the European Communities.

The opposite number to the Common Market, and preceding it in its formation, is the communist Council for Mutual Economic Aid, founded in 1949. The members are Bulgaria, Czechoslovakia, East Germany, Hungary, Mongolia, Poland, Romania, the USSR and, as of 1972, Yugoslavia and Cuba. China, North Korea and North Vietnam have the right to send observers, but never do so nowadays. Obviously this organization is heavily dominated by the USSR, and sometimes there are signs of resentment at this. COMECON nevertheless plays a significant part in the world's economy. As in the defence sphere, so in the economic and commercial, it would be mutually beneficial if the EEC and COMECON could get closer together.

THE COMMONWEALTH

There are twenty-eight full members of the Commonwealth at the present time, plus a few dependent territories (see appendix 3). Literally the only thing they have in common is the fact that

[1] A useful operation for all concerned, on both sides of the fence, would be the setting up of EEC embassies to administer aid to the developing countries.

they were all once part of the British Empire. Some people nurture illusions that one day the Commonwealth will come closer together and form another super-power; but in practice this is out of the question because of the widely disparate situations of the members, some belonging to the first world, others to the second and third, and one or two, such as Tanzania, leaning towards the Chinese sphere. Moreover, the number of members is still dwindling, the latest countries to leave being Sri Lanka and Pakistan. The association is nevertheless well worth while as a body for consultation, trade and aid, and it still holds together a good deal better than many, whether of its members or from outside, expected. It is right that Britain should as far as was practicable have safeguarded its members' privileges in negotiating her entry into EEC; but the overriding consideration had to be that of entry into a body of far greater practical significance than the Commonwealth.

PUGWASH AND OTHERS

A bit of private enterprise that deserves an honourable mention is the Pugwash Conference. This gathering of scientists and politicians from West and East was conceived by Bertrand Russell in 1954 and financed by millionaire Cyrus Eaton on one condition: that it first met in his Nova Scotia home town with that elegant name. In 1971 more than 150 representatives, including Nobel prizewinners, from thirty-two countries met in Bucarest for the twenty-first conference, and were warmly welcomed by President Ceauşescu. The main subject, as usual, was the nuclear arms race; and Pugwash can claim, with some justification, to have helped to lead up to SALT.

A less successful effort is the International Society for World Government. At its inaugural meeting in July 1971 in Trafalgar Square it boasted one speaker, the caption ISOWORG in letters the height of a man, and alas no audience except the pigeons.

There is no space here for details of the scores of other multilateral organizations which, if less significant than those I have mentioned, still play an important part in contemporary diplomacy. Their number, incidentally, is still likely to increase. But perhaps I have said enough to show, broadly, two things. One is that a wide variety of organizations exists which attempt to provide checks and balances in the vital spheres of economic, defence and diplomatic relations. They are never perfect, but in many cases they are a great deal better than nothing. The other point they illustrate is the sheer complexity of the tasks with which diplomacy will have to cope in the 1970s and beyond.

CHAPTER TWELVE

The *modus operandi*

I present a fictional but feasible account of three British diplomats at work.

A NEWCOMER TO THE SERVICE

John Edmondson has just passed the exam for the Diplomatic Service and has been appointed as a third secretary to the Near Eastern department in the FCO. Jack, as his friends call him, was at a grammar school and got a decent II(1) in modern languages at Lancaster University. His family is a conventional middle-middle class one with enough money to live on but none to spare. He came near to winning an exhibition to Cambridge but did not quite pull it off. As candidates are allowed to take only one language in the diplomatic entrance exam he chose his best, Spanish, and did well in it. He also speaks French and German, and one of his main reasons for going for the Diplomatic was his hope that his languages will prove useful and that he can learn some others, in particular Russian. His manner has a hint of shyness about it; his clothes are only reasonably sharp and will get thorough wear. He intends to play hockey at weekends and squash when possible. He is elated at the prospect of over £1,500 a year (it was £275 in my day). He is twenty-four. His family antecedents and his general reliability of character have been thoroughly (or as the FCO puts it, 'positively') vetted before his acceptance.

On this Monday, his first day in the office, elation has given way to nervousness. He arrives promptly at 9 a.m. and is taken along by an avuncular attendant to see the head of his department, who is not yet there. Jack will soon learn that 9.30 a.m. is quite early enough: this gives the channel packet's load of diplomatic bags time to reach the office from Dover by horse-drawn vehicle or British Rail, whichever is the faster. However, the head of department, a counsellor in his early forties called Robens, turns up before long and gives him an affable welcome. Jack calls him sir, but he will be tactfully discouraged from doing this after a short time. He will soon be Jack to Robens, and after a decent interval Robens will be Percy to him. Jack is handed over to one of the two assistant heads of the department, a smart (in all senses of the word) old Etonian called Raymond Watkinson who will bearlead him and generally take him under his wing. These two assistants are first secretaries; and Watkinson introduces Jack to the three colleagues with whom he will share the 'third room', two of them second secretaries and one other third. Jack's desk has a blessedly neat and paperless look which it will not preserve for long. He is to deal with Iran: could be worse, as the department also covers Iraq, Israel, Jordan, Lebanon, Syria, the Central Treaty Organization and the United Nations Relief and Works Agency (UNRWA). Jack is also introduced to the typists in the pool which serves Near Eastern department, and the registry clerks who classify, enter and produce to the department the papers on which they go to work. At this point Watkinson, after inviting Jack to lunch at the Travellers' Club, leaves him to be instructed by an expert clerk, for the whole basis of the department's business and functioning is here. It is easier to do without a good third or second secretary than a good registry clerk.

This seasoned official explains how all communications mainly concerned with Iran will be classified, registered, cross-referenced and submitted, together with any relevant past papers, to Jack. The covers will bear indications both of the urgency of any paper, from 'most immediate' to 'routine', and of its security rating from top secret to open. The registry clerk explains that there will be occasional variations in the procedure: the assistant head of department has made certain delicate subjects his own concern, and a real emergency matter, or one of the highest secrecy, might be handled direct by the head of department or even the assistant under-secretary above him. The registry clerk encourages Jack to ask him whenever he thinks he needs more back papers or cross-references to papers entered with another department. By the time he has shown him several specimen series of papers Jack's lunch appointment is upon him.

The clerk promises to have a good pile of reading matter on the most important current questions affecting Iran deposited on Jack's desk by two o'clock.

Watkinson offers him a gin and tonic in the frivolously decorated bar of the otherwise ponderous Travellers'. Here about half the senior members of the FCO appear to be collected, in no way deterred by having stared at each other's faces in official surroundings from continuing the same ploy unofficially. When Jack is well dug into his roast beef and glass of Beaujolais, Watkinson delivers a little homily on the *modus operandi* of the department, not too pompously. Jack is to do nothing, for the rest of his first week, but read papers on burning Iranian topics, and particularly those descending from the highest levels after decisions have been taken. He is not expected to submit a single minute, comment or suggestion. He is to study both the matter and the mechanics, and he is welcome to consult Watkinson whenever necessary. He is also to familiarize himself with the workings of the communications department; and to make personal contact with his opposite numbers in the North African department, covering all the littoral countries from Egypt to Morocco, plus Sudan, and also with members of the oil department. Watkinson will also give him the names of people in the Department of Trade and Industry and the Ministry of Defence with whom he should go and discuss Iranian matters of concern to those ministries.

After a week he will be let loose on his first very own papers. There are various basic essentials to his work, which he will learn by experience. One is to sort out which questions are urgent or important—not always the same thing—and likely to percolate high up in the hierarchy, and to get a move on with these. Another is to make sure that he has all the relevant past papers; and that other departments of the FCO—not forgetting the legal advisers' department—as well as other government departments with any interest in a particular matter, are given an early opportunity of commenting if they wish. Then whenever possible he should make a constructive proposal for action: this includes 'initialling a paper off' or 'X-ing' it because no action is needed. The days of long, beautifully polished minutes leading nowhere in particular are over. He should try his hand at a draft

telegram or letter wherever appropriate, consulting Watkinson
first by word of mouth if he wishes. There is all too much
paperasserie about; the object is to keep papers moving to their
proper goal. He should use the telephone freely, though not
recklessly. On occasions it may be best to go and discuss something personally in, say, the Department of Trade and Industry;
and he must be prepared before long to play his part in one or
more of the all too numerous committees which operate in
Whitehall. Jack is grateful for, and encouraged by, all this advice.
That evening he returns to his modest flatlet a happier and a
wiser man. The following evening he gives a celebration dinner
to his girlfriend, somewhat overstressing the secrecy of certain
parts of his work to cloak the fact that actually they are none too
clear to him at this stage.

Jack puts his heart into his reading and into establishing his
contacts, and a week later he is raring to go on his own. For the
next few weeks he hesitates to put his initials, as distinct from
his full name, on any papers except when they seem obviously
trivial, and submits the great majority of them to Watkinson,
with drafts of telegrams, letters or memoranda where appropriate. Jack has never been to Iran, or to the Near East come to
that, and he finds the task absorbing: the telegrams reporting
political shifts inside the country and in its foreign policy, the
despatches and letters describing the background scene and reporting significant snippets of information, economic reports
entered with the oil department but sent to him for comment. He
is gratified when an occasional draft by him goes as far as a
deputy under-secretary, the Permanent Under-Secretary, or even
the Secretary of State, and after despatch comes back to him with
marks of their approval. Every day he reads such telegrams and
other papers concerning other parts of the world as are circulated
to his department for general information; so that if one day he
were suddenly switched to, say, the European integration department he would not be totally ignorant of the state of play as
regards the EEC and EFTA.

Watkinson is always encouraging, and makes a point of sending Jack from time to time with a paper to see Robens, who in
turn, though less frequently, sends him on to the assistant under-
secretary. After a few months Watkinson tactfully tells Jack that

he could with advantage 'initial off' more of the less weighty papers; and soon after he unfortunately misjudges the importance of one of these and it has to be rescued from oblivion in connection with a newly arisen crisis. An excitement one day when he is working late and his seniors cannot be contacted is a telephone call from H.M. Ambassador at Teheran about a dangerous political crisis that has brewed up suddenly. He records His Excellency's remarks and takes the record to the Secretary of State's private secretary, who clearly approves of his industry and promptitude though, in accordance with the cardinal diplomatic principle of '*surtout, pas trop de zèle*', he does not go overboard in showing his appreciation. A few months later Jack is sent to attend courses in public administration and economics at the Treasury Centre for Administrative Studies in Regent's Park. He is not over-enthusiastic about these aspects of his work, but recognizes their value. All this time he has been making friends socially with people both in and outside the office, eating and drinking a bit more, going around with a variety of girlfriends.

The great day arrives when Jack is told that his period of probation has been satisfactorily surmounted, and he can expect a posting abroad in a month or two. He is now an established diplomat. On the strength of this he takes out his current favourite girlfriend for quite a night of it, and proposes to her. He points out, fairly enough, that they may well have to go to the ends of the earth; the old 'inner circle' of Paris, Rome and Madrid is out of date, and he would not have qualified for it socially in any case. When the posting comes it is neither too gruelling nor too attractive, and of considerable diplomatic importance: the embassy at Djakarta in Indonesia. His fiancée, who is more than vague about the place, does not hesitate. They are young and they can take it. After several farewell parties, including a small one given by Percy Robens, Jack Edmondson and his new wife are launched on the sea of diplomacy.

A CONSUL-GENERAL

Frank Fanshawe is a horse of a different colour. For a start he is just twice Jack's age, forty-eight. He is Consul-General at Istanbul and has risen to grade four. Satisfactory, some would say; but in fact his career has had some hiccoughs. A double First at Oxford, he started brilliantly and received early promotion. He married happily and two children arrived by the time he was thirty-five. With one exception, and that at the start when it was easiest to endure, his posts abroad have been pleasant enough. But Frank has a somewhat volatile character. The business of moving small children around became a bit of a bore to him. Round about the age of forty, that dangerous time, he began to allow his eye to rove. He made a habit of drinking more than he should at the endless series of cocktail, lunch and dinner parties. He worked fast, as always, but not very long hours. This did not pass unnoticed by his heads of mission or by the personnel department in the Foreign Office. His promotion slowed down. His divorce and remarriage to a charming girl, who happened to be Italian, did him no good; neither divorce nor foreign wives appeal much to the authorities, though they are far more reasonable about such matters than they used to be. He was requested by the powers that be to pull himself together; and, sensibly, he did so. But where he had hoped for promotion to grade four and perhaps a small embassy of his own, what he got was the promotion all right, at the reasonable but not outstanding age of forty-eight, and the Istanbul consulate-general—important as such but kept under the eye of the ambassador in Ankara. He was told that he would probably stay there some five years.

Istanbul, once, as Constantinople, capital of half the world, is today a conglomerate of ancient and modern, picturesque and sordid, the rich and the very poor. No view is more beautiful than that of the Bosporus and the Golden Horn; at the same time you cannot fail to see various forms of pollution on a large scale, or to feel that sinister people and happenings are to be found round every corner. The Fanshawes installed themselves in the large official flat, forming part of the enormous old summer embassy, in what is now one of the noisiest and dirtiest parts of the city. They also rented a small house on the Sea of Marmara, and here they spent many agreeably refreshing weekends.

Frank had only to walk downstairs to his office; and though this arrangement could be annoying in a crisis it also pandered to his tendency to laziness. He seldom arrived at his desk before ten, and his working afternoon often began at a leisurely hour after a post-prandial nap, and seldom extended to more than two hours. The fact was that, while the work offered considerable variety, there was not all that much of it that his good staff of two consuls and four vice-consuls could not deal with. In particular, two locally born vice-consuls knew the ins and outs of the scene admirably. Frank was mainly interested in the political and information sides; but here he was somewhat frustrated, for on those sides he was very much subordinated to the embassy in Ankara. Only rarely did some local political occurrence justify a telegram direct to London, which in every case he would have to repeat to Ankara. Usually he reported direct to Ankara, and the embassy decided whether to make use of his report or not. The Fanshawes circulated freely among the large consular corps, but the pickings in the way of political information were not rich. Frank soon learnt that about 80 per cent of the 'top secret' stuff muttered to him in a corner, by some colleague who had button-holed him for the purpose, was likely to be sheer rumour or fantasy. Istanbul has always been a world centre for espionage and intrigue, and the SIS man who operated in the embassy in Ankara under the innocent-seeming guise of a first secretary made fairly frequent visits to Istanbul. Frank enjoyed the liveliness of this character and the titbits of intelligence which he passed on to him. But while the spook was in duty bound to tell Frank of any little ploys which might possibly cause local complications, he was not in any way controlled by Frank, but by the ambassador and his own head office in London.

Frank's other duties were in the main a good deal less glamorous. First and foremost he had to look after the interests of the British community, whether resident or transient. His duties covered a very wide range, connected with birth, marriage and death. He added to the community by registering new British nationals and births; he married people; he issued passports and visas; he administered relief, and repatriation to Britain, when the occasion arose. He intervened with the Turkish authorities when British citizens were in trouble; and as Istanbul is right on the hippie pot trail this took up quite a bit of his time. He found the Turkish officials, and indeed the Turks generally, pretty dour and sometimes maddening sticklers for the formalities. Yet as time passed and he got to know them better, slowly slowly as they have it, he came to admire and feel affection for some of their qualities, which resemble some of the better features of the British character. He kept up to date a plan for the evacuation of British subjects in an emergency; and made arrangements for burials or the despatch of corpses to Britain, as well as supervising the care of the cemeteries in which British citizens were buried. He also performed all such services for citizens of Commonwealth countries who had no consular representative of their own in the region. Once a year, on the Queen's official birthday, he gave a garden party to a large but selected number of the British community: even the careful selection could not prevent the occasional kooky old lady from removing all her clothes, the professional drunks from getting drunk, and the marginal cases who were not invited from going around grumbling like hell for weeks before and afterwards. And of course in a large port like Istanbul the drunken seaman syndrome was prominent—by which I mean that popular view of a consul's duties that he spends most of his time dealing with such people, whereas in reality he is called upon to perform all kinds of helpful services for British seamen and ships, from signing the men on and off to inspecting the ships or taking delivery of their documents when they are in port for forty-eight hours or more. A varied life; but one in which he was massively helped by his staff.

The other important sectors concerned commerce and information. For each of these he had the backing of a senior consul of first secretary rank who knew his job thoroughly. In the commercial sphere the consulate-general's job was to help advise British businessmen who came to consult them, and also to advise Turks and others interested in trade with Britain; and for these purposes they had to keep themselves fully briefed on commercial and economic developments at both ends. On the information front their activities were both positive and negative. Positively, they tried to present by contacts with Turkish and other journalists an up-to-the-minute picture of Britain, of life as she is lived there, and of British activities and interests in the world. On the defensive side they would answer any snide or denigratory statements about British policy and its execution emanating from any of the communications media. In both cases good, frank relations with local British journalists were by no means the least important factor. In both cases, too, it was desirable to be well up with the field, if not in advance of it. In all his activities Frank of course kept in the closest touch with Ankara, including driving up there every two months or so. He and his wife were always kindly received by the ambassador and ambassadress, who in their turn visited Istanbul about every six months.

After a year at the post both Frank and Donatella felt ready for the leave to which they were entitled, six weeks to be divided between Florence and the Isle of Wight. Frank also, of course, called on the FCO and the DTI and went for a quick week's tour round certain factories which were particularly interested in the Turkish market. At the personnel department he received approbation but also an indication that the job would, as predicted, be a fairly long hard slog. And at the end of a good, refreshing holiday, back to the Istanbul grindstone in time for Frank's number two to take his own well-earned leave. Frank is now rather more enthusiastic about the place and the job than he had been a year before. Donatella still has her doubts, chiefly because of the noise and the dirt. But they are happy together, and both prepared to brave out a few more years there if needs be. Soon they will be speculating: what next? As Frank will be in his early fifties promotion would be nice; then he could have his own little embassy, or be an assistant under-secretary supervising two or three departments in London. They could see more of their various children. But promotion is far from certain. At the same time he will be a bit long in the tooth to be a mere head of department. So it looks like either another consulate-general, or a tiny embassy in a perhaps uninviting place, or a counsellor's job in a large embassy. Time, and the personnel operations department, will tell.

A TOP AMBASSADOR

In some ways the mode of life of His Excellency Sir William Wiseman, KCMG, KCVO, is out of this world; yet as H.M. Ambassador in Washington he is right at the centre of the world of affairs. He is of course used by now to being Ambassador Extraordinary and Plenipotentiary; and the demands of displaying his excellency are nothing new to him. He is a Knight Commander of the Order of St Michael and St George because he has worked his way up to grade one of the Diplomatic Service; and in his eminence in the top grade he can look forward confidently to his 'G', in other words to becoming a Knight Grand Cross of the Order. He is in addition Knight Commander of the Royal Victorian Order by luck: he happened to be ambassador in Chile when the Sovereign, in whose gift that order lies, paid an official visit to that country. He is fifty-eight and has a couple more years in the Service before retirement. Sir William and Lady Wiseman live in the palace built by Lutyens in none too inspiring a style, and there are quite a few rooms in it which they will never see. They have virtually unlimited staff, both official and domestic.

Sir William's senior official staff numbers about eighty, including four ministers, a lieutenant-general, a rear-admiral, an air vice-marshal and counsellors galore. These eighty constitute the tip of the iceberg, and it is natural that only by chance can the Ambassador come to know personally anyone below the heads of sections—the counsellor who is head of chancery and thus responsible for general co-ordination; the ministers heading the commercial, economic and defence research and development sections; the head of the British defence staff who is also defence attaché, and so on. Also under the Ambassador's overall control are a couple of dozen consulates-general and consulates, some as far-flung as the Pacific Islands, Honolulu, Puerto Rico and Alaska. Their incumbents will be lucky if they ever clap eyes on their chief. What an apparatus! It has the impersonality of a large firm. Some of the counsellors are not sure where the others have their offices, let alone where those of the more junior staff are to be found. It is not surprising that it is criticized from time to time in Parliament and the press as being excessive and unwieldy.

Sir William is a businesslike and modern-minded man. In addition to his top Diplomatic Service salary of just under £16,000 he receives tax-free *frais de représentation* of about £20,000 per year. He does not manage to save much, although he tries to cut down purely diplomatic entertaining which tends to bore him, and his wife even more, to a decent minimum. He begins his working day at nine o'clock by reading through the numerous telegrams received from all over the world, and also any personal and/or top secret letters and despatches which may have just arrived. At half past nine his deputy, 'the Minister' *tout court*, and the nine heads of section assemble, and when 'H.E.', as he is called, is ready they go in to him. He attributes great importance to this daily meeting. He expects his staff to tell him succinctly but comprehensively of new developments of significance in their sections, and to add constructive comments and cross-comments. He himself will give instructions for action and set a time-scale in each case. The meeting may last half an hour or extend to an hour; it is always time well spent. H.E. is not the old-fashioned type of ambassador who sets store by elegance of style and lengthy minutes and records on every topic. What he looks for is the appropriate action, taken at the appropriate speed. God help the laggard, or on the other hand the over-smart aleck who misses out a vital point.

Among the numerous telegrams two marked 'most immediate' have arrived from the FCO, having been dispatched five hours later by local London time. They concern Berlin and Vietnam respectively. Sir William gives instructions on the general lines of the reply on Berlin, to be submitted to him the same afternoon as soon as some necessary research among past papers has been done. The Vietnam message raises such crucial points, on which replies will have to be made to a parliamentary question (or p.q.) next day, that he rings up the US Secretary of State and asks whether he could see him for twenty minutes some time the same day. The Secretary of State has an official lunch, and so has the Ambassador; but a meeting is arranged for 3 p.m. In order to check up on one or two top secret points the Ambassador sends for his head spy. He masquerades as one of the numerous counsellors, although his identity is fully known to the rest of the senior staff, to the American State Department, the CIA and the FBI, as well as to the leading local communist diplomats and spies and of course to the KGB in Moscow. His job is not to spy on our US allies—well, not much, anyway—but to maintain close liaison with the CIA and the FBI. Some of our older and stuffier ambassadors to this day look down their noses at the activities of DI6, but Sir William is not one of those. He likes the original turn of mind of the local representative, and finds that the intelligence he supplies is often useful.

The diplomatic lunch, at the Portuguese ambassador's residence, is as crashingly boring as Sir William had expected. But he is trained to endure such things. The brandy-drinking and cigars are still flourishing when he takes his leave, so as to arrive at the Secretary of State's office just before three o'clock. The Secretary of State, a large, genial man, has had an equally tedious assignment, and they commiserate with each other. The points which the Ambassador is under instruction to raise are rather thorny, and in spite of his great diplomatic skill and the good personal relations between the two men the interview is not an easy one, and goes on for over half an hour. Then Sir William returns to his office and dictates his 'most immediate' telegraphic reply to London, reporting on the nuances of the discussion and giving his own recommendations on how the points at issue should be handled in the public forum. While he is waiting for the dictation to be typed out he switches his mind to the draft telegram on the Berlin question, which the Minister has submitted. It is, as usual from that quarter, an efficient composition and H.E. initials it off without hesitation. Having also sent his own telegram on Vietnam for despatch he can at last get down to some routine reading, which even ambassadors must do if they are to keep abreast of the vast spectrum of problems concerning them. There is an important background despatch about the negotiations for Britain's entry into the Common Market; there is a report on the latest developments in Ulster, with great potential significance for British–US relations; there is a commercial report of some weight from the consulate-general at San Francisco; there is even a short but probing report from the embassy's administration section on the subject of rents of diplomats' houses and offices. All these are filtered through the Minister, who is himself a KCMG of great experience and an ex-ambassador at a junior post, and it is very seldom indeed that H.E. feels he is being troubled with any paper or discussion unnecessarily.

Fortunately, H.E. and Lady Wiseman are that evening only giving a semi-formal party for some middle-piece staff, counsellors and so on, and their opposite numbers from the State Department and the French and West German embassies. Sir William enjoys this type of party for a change, though he would not have said no to an entirely free evening, a rarity indeed. But after a bath, with a fortifying whisky and water to hand, and a change, though not this evening into black tie, he feels restored and ready for the fray. The American wife on his right at dinner is a good-looker and the food and wine are up to the usual pretty fair standard—broadly speaking better than that of the Americans but not up to French standards. The guests do not linger, and he is finishing his nightcap and looking forward to bed when the telephone rings. The Minister, with many apologies, asks whether he could come round for five minutes in connection with Vietnam. H.E. agrees, and indeed the new piece of information which the Minister has picked up at a dinner party that evening is of considerable significance and relevance to the p.q. The Minister has brought a further draft 'most immediate' telegram to London and the Ambassador approves it, with thanks. The communications section despatches it immediately. It is 11.45 p.m., and the Ambassador is more than ready to sleep.

When the time comes, some two years later, for Sir William and Lady Wiseman to retire he duly receives his GCMG. Four out of the last five ambassadors at Washington have gone on to receive peerages, but after further services to the state. The Wisemans decide that they have had enough of public life, though he accepts a couple of part-time directorships in the City. They have a pleasant but not imposing house in the home counties, and enough to live on comfortably though not luxuriously. The contrast with their lives as part of the diplomatic apparatus is of course enormous. There is the pension, ample but not viceregal, with no tax-free allowances; one part-time domestic servant, and no able ministers and private secretaries; the drink about four times as expensive as before. It is, as Lady Wiseman puts it, the transition from mink to sink. They are invited to occasional diplomatic dinners; but in this direction too they feel they have had about enough. Sir William toys with the idea of writing his memoirs; he is dissuaded, infinitely gently and tactfully, by his wife on the sound grounds that only about one book in twenty written by retired British ambassadors in their sixties is remotely readable. The Wisemans have played a full and distinguished part in Britain's diplomacy. Now they are

happy to cultivate their family, their personal rather than diplomatic friends, and their garden.

TWO REAL-LIFE CAREERS

Finally, it is worth looking at a couple of real-life careers, one
exceptional and the other normally successful. The present Permanent Under-Secretary of State at the FCO and Head of the
Diplomatic Service, Sir Denis Arthur Greenhill, has had an
admirably unconventional career. This man did not enter the
Foreign Office until he was thirty-two, in 1945. He received his
CMG at the age of forty-six—good but not brilliant. He was still
a counsellor at forty-nine. At fifty-three he got his K; but at
fifty-five he was Permanent Under-Secretary and all the rest of
it, surging ahead of dozens of far longer-established—and more
pompous—diplomats.

Greenhill comes of an ordinary middle-class family who lived
in a part of Essex which was just beyond the suburbs but is so no
longer. His parents were active Congregationalists. Unlike all
preceding heads of the Foreign Office except one—Lord Strang,
who went to a grammar school—he went not to a smart public
school but to an unfashionable, though worthy, minor one near
by, Bishop's Stortford College. He got into Christ Church,
Oxford, and did his time there without any particular distinction.
He gained a second-class honours degree, which is normal
among senior British diplomats. He had no social connections.
As a career he chose the railways, the nostalgic old London and
North-Eastern to be exact. He did not have time to make a success of this particular career because the war cut it short; but he
certainly made a success of his two others. He fought the war in
the Royal Engineers—not the Guards—from 1939 to 1945, received the Order of the British Empire in 1941, was three times
mentioned in despatches, and ended up as a full colonel at the age
of thirty-one. Not bad going by any means. In the course of his
military career he saw large parts of the world: Egypt, the rest of
north Africa, Italy, India and south-east Asia—a good preparation for his next career.

At the end of 1945 the Foreign Office somewhat grudgingly
'employed' him, as the phrase was, in the department dealing
with oil supplies. On 1 January 1946 he was established in his

employment, as a first secretary. A career of interesting diversity followed. At the end of 1947 he was sent to Sofia, a tricky post in those early cold war times, and was given early responsibility— he acted as chargé d'affaires for a time in both 1948 and 1949. The Bulgarians expelled him for alleged espionage. Still a first secretary, he went to Washington in 1949 for three years and dealt largely with military supplies and co-ordination. He then returned to the Foreign Office for just over a year.

A sign of his success with the Americans was the fact that he was attached to their representative at the coronation of Queen Elizabeth II. I was similarly attached to the Turkish Prime Minister, and I recollect it as a week of pretty gruelling formalities, dressing up in full uniform, and junketings in Buckingham Palace and elsewhere. During 1954 Greenhill was attached to the Imperial Defence College, and this added a dimension to his experience that was to prove valuable. At the age of forty-two, in 1955, he was promoted counsellor and transferred to the British delegation to NATO, thus continuing on the side of diplomacy concerned with strategy as well as politics. The same applied to his next posting to Singapore; and for most of 1959 he added some specialized experience when he succeeded me as Foreign Office adviser to the Chief of the SIS.

Greenhill then returned to Washington as one of the numerous counsellors; and it was here that the breakthrough was to occur. He got on very well with the Americans, which many of our conventional diplomats consider they do, but erroneously. Consequently the Foreign Office took an extremely unusual, but in this case commendable, step. In 1962 he was promoted *sur place* to the position of Minister. In passing, it would be no bad thing if this were done more often: an efficient diplomat who knows the local scene can frequently be more valuable than a stranger of higher rank who has to spend a year or so learning all about it. So there was Greenhill, aged just forty-nine, in grade three. In 1964 he returned to the Foreign Office in the same grade, as assistant under-secretary, having won golden opinions.

Two more great leaps forward followed. In 1966, although a fairly junior member of grade three, he was promoted to grade two as deputy under-secretary in charge of all the Foreign Office's strategic thinking and collaboration with the armed and intelligence services. Here again he performed doughtily for nearly three years, getting on well with the Labour ministers in charge. And to the chagrin, it must frankly be said, of many of the longer-established officials, he was promoted many places on the list by George Brown to follow two successive Etonians in his present highly responsible post in February 1969. If all goes normally he should continue in it until 1973.

Greenhill would not strike anyone today as an unconventional diplomat; nor has he ever displayed striking originality. His only club is that annexe of the FCO, the Travellers'. He can be patriarchal, and there is a danger that nearly five years in office may stiffen him up. But up to now he has always been not only efficient but forward-looking, with a broad view of diplomacy which in particular gives due weight to the vital importance of nuclear strategy. His really good relations with Americans are a great asset. He readily collaborated in the deliberate leak which constituted 'the Soames affair' and administered a salutary jolt to de Gaulle; though some more old-fashioned British diplomats and newspapers considered it hardly cricket. He and his deputy and assistant under-secretaries present a much more contemporary and modern-minded appearance than we have had for some time at the headquarters of our foreign relations. Provided that bad old habits and customs do not creep back, and there is a danger that they might, particularly through the influence of some politicians, I can see Greenhill and his colleagues leading British diplomacy responsibly and sensibly through the 1970s.

Not everyone can be as successful in his career as Denis Greenhill. But even without that the diplomat who attains middling seniority can make a valuable contribution as a human being, an efficient operator and a representative of his country. I quote now the career of one whom I know very well, and who is ending up shortly as a consul-general in grade four. He is, as it happens, practically a twin of Greenhill's, comes of similar stock, went to a similar school and also to Oxford. However, on coming down, he went straight for the Consular Service, which was regarded *de haut en bas* by the Diplomatic Service in those days, and won a place in 1938. He was immediately sent out to agreeable Valparaiso in Chile as vice-consul, and instructed to pursue his career when he volunteered for active service on the outbreak of war. In 1940 he very wisely married an attractive and sweet redhead; they have since produced three sons of character and originality, two born in Montevideo and one in Addis Ababa. My friend spent from 1940 to 1946 in Montevideo, a post of some importance in the war, and then three years in the Foreign Office. Here he went well, and became a first secretary at the very reasonable age of thirty-three. As such he was sent, having crossed to the fully 'diplomatic' ladder, to our embassy in Addis Ababa, and acted as chargé d'affaires for a while in each of his four years there. Good going, on the face of it; but he unfortunately fell foul of both the two ambassadors whose right-hand man he was. They were both, as I know personally, tiresome men and one of the wives was a virago into the bargain. Their reports to the personnel department on my friend were consequently not helpful to his career, though they were happy to go away on lengthy holidays and leave him in charge of the embassy. As a result he continued in the same rank of first secretary in two other posts, Innsbrück and Prague, until 1956. Still, he was then promoted counsellor at the age of forty-three, and sent to our embassy in Jedda, Saudi Arabia. Unfortunately he has never, to this day, risen further, though he has done good work in Canberra; as consul-general at Lyons where he was highly popular in both cultural and industrial circles, and was rewarded by being made a CBE; as H.M. Ambassador (but still in grade four) to the Dominican Republic—no picnic, this; and finally as consul-general at Stuttgart.

That is a varied career of valuable service to British diplomacy, a good deal of it carried out in places where for one reason or another most British people would not choose to live. My friend has not been liberally rewarded for that service, certainly not financially. One of his handicaps has probably been the fact that he is an artist: he published a good book of poems when young, he is a well above average painter, he writes for *The Times Literary Supplement*, he is a member of the Athenaeum and the Garrick as well as the PEN. Such gifts have in the past been generally regarded with suspicion by the personnel department; and it must in fairness be said that they sometimes siphon off some of the time and energy which a single-mindedly ambitious diplomat would devote exclusively to his career. My friend would not pretend to be an expert on nuclear strategy or the effect of world liquidity on the balance of payments situation; and it is significant that he has not been required to serve in London, where on the whole names are made in the Service, since 1949. But there is room for all-round human beings like his wife and himself in representing Britain abroad; and it is good that they were not axed in the recent Diplomatic Service purge of some thirty members of about their age and stage, but were asked to continue to give service in their comparatively modest grade.

I do not consider that the career structure of the Diplomatic Service is perfect; nor, fortunately, do the more progressive elements inside the Service. But these brief descriptions of very different careers have perhaps shown in some measure that, apart from the fliers, varied and useful careers can be enjoyed—most of the time—by diplomats who are prepared to do anything, go anywhere.

CHAPTER THIRTEEN

Handling a Crisis

H.M. Ambassador to FCO. Cypher telegram. Confidential. June 17.

I apologize if my numerous telegrams of the past few days have appeared confused. They reflected the situation here. Now that N is safely back in power it is possible to send this round-up.

2. I have little doubt that the abortive coup was communist-inspired. The communist party in this country is relatively well organized, and has been infiltrating the army. The two officers who temporarily left the country as a deliberate tactical move in the plot were closely in touch with the ringleaders. The President escaped only by extreme good luck, and the action of his ally, the President to the north, then enabled him to smash the conspiracy. The President has made his displeasure very clear to the Soviet embassy, and some members of the staff have thought it wise to leave in a hurry.

3. I have congratulated the President on his escape and I see no reason why my relations with him should be impaired, or British interests affected, as a result of these events.

US Ambassador to State Department. Cypher telegram. Secret. June 15.

Doubtless the recent happenings were put-up job by P. Otherwise impossible he escape death, and contrive capture of ringleaders. Q agrees and is reporting in parallel to his head office. He hinted as much to a personal friend close to P who went as near as he dared to confirm. All quiet now and relations with P run along normally. No sort of anti-US feeling has been aroused. For more details, see Q's report.

K to Andropov, KGB Headquarters, Moscow. Special cypher telegram. Top Secret. Immediate. June 12.

Chinese provocation has succeeded all too well. Suspicions I reported in my no. 493 are confirmed. They infiltrated local communist party and it was their stooges who ran the whole show. They have also managed to get the blame put on this embassy and the loyal members of the communist party, some of whom have been shot. Essential we purge local party and reorganize cells and cadres. Also essential to keep sharpest watch on Chinese who are increasing numbers here as President turns towards them and away from us. Here M's cell can be effective if they can preserve their Maoist cover.

2. I have ordered ambassador back to Moscow without delay, and also C, S and Y for good reasons. I propose to return myself shortly and will then discuss future plans. Please approve and send guidance.

French Chargé d'Affaires to Quai d'Orsay. *En clair* telegram. June 14.

President fully back in power, if anything in stronger position than before. Such things happen in these countries. French citizens and interests unharmed. I propose now to take leave which had to be postponed. Polisson will be in charge.

Her Majesty's Principal Secretary of State for Foreign Affairs to H.M. Ambassador. Saving telegram by bag. *En clair*. Restricted. June 25.

Your reports on the recent crisis have been helpful not only as regards the local scene but also in the wider context of the shifts of power in the continent where you are *en poste*. I approve your actions.

2. All my information confirms your judgement that the coup was communist-inspired. This being the case, I shall be glad if you will deliver my personal message of sympathy and con-

gratulation to the President, as set out in my immediately following telegram.

3. Please continue to keep a sharp eye on communist activities, not only Russian but Chinese.

Secretary of State to US Ambassador. Cypher telegram. Top Secret. June 18.

Your interpretation of motivation of recent crisis may be right but intelligence received from sources other than Q's suggest alternative possibilities of possibly great significance. Will telegraph again after next meeting of National Security Council where whole matter is to be evaluated.

Z Moscow to K. Personal. Decypher yourself. Special cypher telegram. Top Secret. Immediate. June 14.

This is very serious setback.

2. I approve your action on ambassador, C, S and Y. You will however await at your post instructions being sent in near future by hand of special courier G. These concern once-for-all action by you in connection with cells, and you should be prepared to return here the moment you have taken it.

3. You should not, repeat not, inform Chargé d'Affaires of any details. I have informed Gromyko on personal basis of what he needs to know.

Quai d'Orsay to French Chargé d'Affaires. *En clair* telegram. June 17.

Your telegram of June 14. *D'accord.*

CHAPTER FOURTEEN

Some proposals

In this chapter I propose to recapitulate some aspects of the probable shape and form of diplomacy in the 1970s; and to offer some proposals of my own designed, I hope, to make the apparatus better able to cope with the complex problems which we have examined.

TODAY'S DIPLOMAT

What personal qualifications will be required of the diplomat in the future? It may seem odd, but I believe it would be difficult to improve on Allen Dulles' list, compiled ten years ago, of what he thought were the qualities of a good intelligence officer. These were: 'Be perceptive about people; be able to work well with others under difficult conditions; learn to discern between fact and fiction; be able to distinguish between essentials and non-essentials; possess inquisitiveness; have a large amount of ingenuity; pay appropriate attention to detail; be able to express ideas clearly, briefly and, very important, interestingly; learn when to keep your mouth shut. . . . He must have an understanding for other points of view, other ways of thinking and behaving, even if they are quite foreign to his own.' Needless to say, the good diplomat does not have to be an intellectual, an aristocrat or a rich man; for a generation now few British diplomats have been any of these. Miles Copeland, who knows well the workings of the CIA, commented, I think in jest, that all the top Agency men were disinterested operators because they were wealthy. Perhaps in some cases the word might be 'irresponsible'. More seriously, he writes: 'The ideal diplomat is one who can regard all frustrations and handicaps, including misjudgements of superiors, as a doctor faces human ailments: not as evils to inveigh against but as components of problems to be solved with a cool head.'

This list of qualities is a formidable and a fundamental one, to which I should like to add a brief list of the kinds of attitude which will prove positively unhelpful. One is to hark back to Harold Nicolson and Lord Strang and talk about the eternal verities of diplomacy and some inflexible form of apparatus. In the press, such headlines as 'King Hussein hits out for the Royal Amman Cricket Club against the British embassy', and 'A four in the East–West bridge game' on the deadly serious question of Berlin, are mischievously frivolous. At the other end of the spectrum the mechanistic ideas of some worshippers of computers and diplomatic scenarios are apt to be dangerously rigid, though such methods can help on certain occasions and up to a certain point. In the 1970s our diplomats should forget more about British traditions, and concentrate instead on a flexible approach to future probable and possible developments. Each nation's capabilities and aspirations vary, in different degrees, from year to year and even more from decade to decade. A good diplomat should bear in mind that there are always at least three possible ways of dealing with a situation: take action to affect it in a positive sense; ditto, but in a negative sense; or do nothing about it. On most big issues the last course is not to be recommended; but there are occasions which call for 'masterly inactivity'. In this connection, what of the think-tank techniques? A certain amount of forward planning for various contingencies is obviously desirable, and the amount now existing in the FCO might be increased with advantage in order to sharpen up our readiness to cope with possible developments. This might take the form of a small body of both officials and politicians directly under the Foreign Secretary or his senior minister of state. But the lesson of the Pentagon Papers is a dreadful warning that the process can easily be carried much too far.

THE DIPLOMATIC CAREER

How best, then, to recruit people with these qualities for the British Diplomatic Service? The net is undoubtedly thrown wider than it was a few years ago, but I still feel that a greater effort could and should be made, just as the armed forces have in their efforts to recruit a higher level of candidate. It should not hesitate to advertise in order to put across a contemporary, and forward-looking, image and thus appeal to the sort of people it needs. Not least should the FCO emphasize that it now organizes far more serious training in administration, business methods and languages than ever before, such as using the Harvard Business School; and that such training will be obligatory not only at the outset of a career but also in the form of refresher courses at intervals throughout it. In the case of languages, of course, the more that any one diplomat can master, the better. A year or two ago the Foreign Office had, in round figures, 125 qualified Russian speakers, 60 Japanese, 55 Chinese, 45 Persian, 30 Turkish and 30 Polish. I trust that these numbers have by now considerably increased, and will go on increasing. At the same time, I think that we would profit from abolishing the pretence that French is any longer the *lingua franca* of diplomacy. A beautiful language, of course; but for practical purposes it has no right to rank above Anglo-American, Russian, Chinese, Japanese and Spanish.

We have seen that career prospects have in many ways been improved and made more flexible. I should like to see the process carried further and faster. To put it in an extreme fashion, it should be open to every typist and clerk to become an ambassador; though obviously this cannot mean that they will all do so. In addition, arrangements should be made for the real fliers to reach grade two, or even grade one, by the age of forty. This occurs in the home Civil Service. Such a system would often result in the fliers leaving for other occupations by, say, fifty; and I can see positive advantage in this not only for the Diplomatic Service itself, in that promotion would be hastened for others, but for the profession or industry to which the still youngish diplomat could devote his talents, and even for him personally. Nobody in the 1970s should think in terms of less than two careers in a lifetime.

In return, a career in the Diplomatic Service should be presented as something more adventurous than is the case at present, and less of a steady, guaranteed Civil Service grind through to the age of sixty. Every entrant should be fairly warned that his or her record will be thoroughly scrutinized at the age of forty and again at fifty, with the idea of a possible termination of their diplomatic career; and even if the fifty mark is successfully passed there would be no guarantee of more than one further post. In all cases generous compensation should be paid. These measures would keep people on their toes. The present compulsory retiring age of sixty should be strictly maintained, not least with the object of developing a younger Service. And every diplomat's career should include a spell in the Ministry of Defence and another in the Department of Trade and Industry. It is also important that as many members of the Service as possible should at some stage serve as international civil servants on the staff of one or more of the numerous multinational organizations. In the past the tendency has been to shuffle people off to such posts when the personnel administration could not think what else to do with them. This is a mistake: many such jobs are both important, demanding and educative.

In short, our Diplomatic Service and FCO should aim at being a highly trained *corps d'élite*, though not, of course, in any social sense. The more I think about the proposed 'slenderization', the more important it seems. Anthony Barber let slip, in a parliamentary answer which was intended to defend the Queen's emoluments, that they amounted to only a little more than the cost of running our embassy in Washington. Surprisingly, no one took the obvious point that the expense of the embassy is thus shown to be preposterous, and should be severely pruned.

Nor should the FCO be complacent about salary scales, much improved though these have recently become. Miles Copeland, senior partner in Scope International Inc., pointed out in the British press that a service like his paid 'roughly double the salaries offered by the FCO, plus conspicuously more comfortable and bureaucracy-free travel and living accommodation'. His employees then included three former Foreign Office men; and a flow of applications from others immediately ensued.

WOMEN IN DIPLOMACY

W. H. Auden writes: 'Today our phallic toys have become too dangerous to be tolerated. I see little hope for a peaceful world until men are excluded from the realm of foreign policy altogether, and all decisions concerning international relations are reserved for women, preferably married ones.' I fear that this shows how the poet's world differs from the real one: three of the most aggressive prime ministers in the world are married women. But joking apart, the British Diplomatic Service still makes no serious effort to recruit women and offer them proper career prospects, although it is quite certain that there are various jobs and situations with which they can cope at least as effectively as men. There are just nine women among the 501 senior staff in the top four grades, none of them in the top two. I do not even see why they should be forced to resign on marriage if they consider that they can carry on. One great Soviet ambassador, and one good American one, were married women who carried out highly important missions with success.

WELFARE

The welfare of our diplomats, in the broadest sense, has received far more attention in recent years; but even today it seems necessary for individuals and groups in the Service to put pressure on the authorities, rather than the latter adopting a liberal and imaginative line. 'Welfare' is quoted in the FCO list as just one subject in a total of twenty-two handled by four separate administrative departments. I should have thought it merited a department on its own. One voluntary group that does good work in this direction is the Diplomatic Service Wives' Association; yet this was only founded as recently as 1965. The administrative authorities should realize that you cannot get diplomats, let alone consuls in outlying and perhaps disagreeable posts, to work happily, and hence efficiently, unless the highly unusual problems facing their wives and children, which are bound to crop up in various posts during any normal career, are handled sympathetically and effectively.

A NEW REPORT ON THE DIPLOMATIC SERVICE

This leads me to my next proposal. When I asked a top official in the FCO whether a heart-searching report, similar to the American Macomber report, was likely to be produced by members of our Diplomatic Service about that Service, his reply was twofold: that morale in our Service was much higher than in the US Foreign Service; and that our Service had been pretty thoroughly reported upon at short intervals in recent years. Consequently he did not consider that a further inspection was necessary. I beg to differ. The last one, the Duncan report, was delivered in 1969; it was drawn up in a hurry by three members of the Establishment; it has already been side-tracked in certain respects; and it did not deal in any depth with the FCO because that was not in the terms of reference. George Brown commented: 'I had high hopes of the Duncan Commission. I must record my sad feeling that when I read their report I felt this was possibly the most missed opportunity of several decades to bring about a genuine reform of the Foreign Service. It is a job somebody still has to carry out.' Indeed the FCO has never submitted itself to thorough inspection by anyone outside its ranks. While I would not in any way compare our sensible FCO with the Pentagon, it is of some interest that the latter was inspected for a year by a panel of fourteen people headed by a high-powered business executive and including a labour leader, two lawyers, an academic or two, and a former professional footballer. Incidentally, they concluded: 'Frankly, we think it is an impossible organization to administer. We are amazed that it works at all.'

I have no fear of a similar judgement on our diplomatic apparatus, but I suggest that it would help it as a whole to look ahead if the FCO and the Diplomatic Service abroad were thoroughly inspected by a team of complete 'outsiders', or ordinary intelligent people. This might include a 'housewife', a trade union official, a politician, a scientist, a professional sportsman, a journalist, a public relations officer and so on. A precondition would have to be that our diplomats and other officials were under orders to collaborate whole-heartedly and not to drag their feet. In the region of security, for instance, only the most delicate of top secrets should be withheld. I also think that the SIS could benefit from an outside inspection; though the difficulties here are obvious. The team would do well to consider, among other matters, this comment of Lord Trevelyan's on the Soviet system: 'The Foreign Ministry was directed by the Collegium, a body founded by Peter the Great, with powers laid down by law. We knew little about how it worked, but it probably exercised real authority, at least over the administration of the Ministry and the Foreign Service. There was much to be said for the adoption of a similar system in our FO and there are signs of changes in FO practice in this direction.' My own comment here would be that while a form of the Collegium system might well help us forward, I am pretty certain that in the Soviet form it must contain powerful KGB elements, and we want nothing of that kind in our case.

OFFICES AND HOUSING FOR DIPLOMATS

For the first time in living memory the Foreign Office building has recently had a wash and brush up, surely a hopeful psychological sign. Nevertheless the old comment is still applicable: '*c'est magnifique, mais ce n'est pas la gare*'—of St Pancras, which the building was originally intended to be. It becomes less suitable as a head office all the time: some of the top officials' rooms are almost too grand and thus wasteful of space, while many of those where junior officials and typists have to work are little better than cubby-holes. Besides, it is only one of seventeen buildings scattered around London which constitute the headquarters of the Diplomatic Service. The top officials recognize sheepishly that the situation is ridiculous, wasteful and unworthy. It is more than high time that some powerful characters were instructed to spend their whole time throwing their weight about until it is remedied. Lord Trevelyan's comment is apposite: 'Nor could there be a greater difference between the Foreign Ministry in Moscow and the FO in London, the one orderly, the corridors of the other stacked with old cupboards and furniture, looking like a disused warehouse in the London docks.'

There is also serious cause for complaint about the embassy and chancery buildings which have been built in the last twenty years. One newspaper described the lot as 'showing a second-best flag'; and if our diplomatic power is no longer what it was, it is surely all the more important that the setting from which it is wielded should be suitably dignified. The dead hand of the old Office of Works lay heavily on the Ministry of Public Building and Works that succeeded it in 1950; and the Directorate of Estate Management Overseas (DEMO) section of the Department of the Environment has not altered all that much in character because of an alteration of title. I have looked at photographs and plans of twenty-two chancery buildings erected since the difficult days of 1953 when the Bonn building, resembling a minor factory in, say, Warwickshire, was put up; they cover posts from Washington through New Delhi, Monrovia, Gaberones, Stockholm, Mbabane, to Islamabad. It seems to me that only Madrid, Islamabad, Brasilia and Sir Basil Spence's Rome (the construction of which was held up for eight years) display any distinction; and a good many people disagree about the last one. The system under which decisions to build are taken by an estates surveyor of the DEMO, who is by definition a dyed-in-the-wool civil servant, and a senior diplomat doing his stint as an FCO inspector, could hardly be better designed to produce mediocre results. I support the idea that competitions open to all, including the DEMO, should be instituted under a separate organization within the FCO financed by the Treasury, rather like the foreign buildings operations section of the State Department in the US. Thus our best designers and architects would have the opportunity of displaying their talents in a worthy cause all round the world.

A related sphere in which the FCO administration needs to get a move on is that of housing for diplomatic staffs abroad. There is too much pointless diversity in different posts, though clearly absolute uniformity in very widely differing conditions is out of the question. Accommodation provided at very high rentals is still rife, and the sooner it is replaced by freehold purchases, or new freehold buildings, the better it will be for all concerned, and not least for the finances of the FCO. (In my last two posts in the Service, when I held ambassadorial rank, I had first to dicker with the army in Cyprus over my quarters, and then to put through on my own initiative the renting of the Berlin residence of the Netherlands ambassador in Bonn.) And it would be good for morale if the FCO played a larger part in finding and financing accommodation for its members and their families when they are serving in London.

SERVICE AT HOME AND ABROAD

What is the ideal spell for a diplomat in any one post? It is impossible to generalize because posts and people differ so fundamentally. Language, climate, local amenities, and all sorts of other considerations come into it. It may be right, for instance, to keep a consul who really knows the local people and language in a post for ten years; though there is always the danger of his 'going native', as the condescending expression used to be. With modern communications that danger is considerably lessened. On average I would say that the present postings of two to three years are rather too short. It takes even a lively diplomat up to a year thoroughly to get the feel of a new job; and it is unsettling if he or she begins soon after that to start casting an eye over the list of future possibilities. Broadly, therefore, I would suggest that three full years should be the minimum, four perfectly normal, and five or a little more in no way exceptional particularly in the senior ranks, whether in London or abroad. There has been some movement in this direction, and it is to be welcomed.

THE STRUCTURE OF THE SERVICE

I have considerable criticisms to make of the structure of the FCO, though in fairness I must say that the top administrators seem to be trying to rationalize it all the time. However, at my moment of writing, it has sixty-six departments, which by any standards is far too many. Particularly excessive are the eleven devoted to administrative matters, which can only lead to chaos; the nine dealing with various aspects of information; and the seven with defence and associated subjects. All of these aspects are important, but too much is too much. At the other end of the scale it is highly significant, and unsatisfactory, that only two departments deal, in each case, with American, east European and Soviet and United Nations affairs. The priorities should be put right as soon as possible. Another form of economy which might actually increase efficiency would be to cut down staffs at appropriate posts and deal instead either with the foreign mission in London or at the United Nations. And can it really be necessary to have resident British consuls at places such as Aabenraa, Bacalod, El Cardón and Salta?

AID

I am realistic enough to expect few results from a plea for greatly increased aid to the developing countries. Nevertheless it is worth repeating that this is a really important matter. The 1972 UNCTAD meeting in Santiago achieved some degree of meeting of minds; but it ended in frustration and recriminations on the part of the ninety-six developing nations occasioned by what they regarded as the hypocrisy of the rich. The cause is in every way so much more worth while than, for instance, frittering away millions of pounds on ineffectual defence measures. If rich Western countries will not supply the aid, communist countries will: look at the Aswan dam and the Tanzam railway, not to mention numerous less ambitious projects sponsored by East Germany in a dozen African countries. As a small start the aid section of the FCO should again become a separate ministry with a properly trained staff.

SECURITY

The Diplomatic Service regulations in force at the end of 1970 gave the highest salary attainable by a senior security officer as £1,347 per annum. This was hardly higher than that of a grade ten officer of the diplomatic branch or a grade two member of the secretarial branch. The Service and the FCO have a long tradition of inefficiency and amateurishness on the security side. Now that assassination, abduction and hijacking are here to stay on the diplomatic scene, we really must put more serious efforts into security measures; this means, among other things, paying considerably more for more highly trained and experienced security officers. I do not in the slightest mean to imply that our present body of stout fellows is open to financial suborning. But this sphere is so important that a pinchpenny policy simply will not do. At the worst it could endanger top secrets of cosmic importance. Similarly, there was talk not so long ago of a strike of British diplomatic wireless operators because they are the only people at their salary level who are not given local diplomatic status. The Foreign and Commonwealth Office would be well advised to meet their demands, for the diplomatic apparatus would be hamstrung without them. Their effectiveness and courage in our beleaguered Amman embassy during the Jordanian civil war fully deserved the high praise it received.

A concomitant of this stepping up of positive security is the stepping down of the aged Official Secrets Acts. There have been more than enough conspicuous examples in court recently of the ridiculous attempts to apply these measures, actions which have failed while causing considerable expense to the taxpayer. Or again cases like this one, which proved 'successful' from the point of view of the security authorities: 'A clerk at the British embassy in Algiers was further remanded in custody on a charge under the Official Secrets Acts. He is alleged, on a date unknown between July 1968 and April 1971 in Khartoum, Sudan, for a purpose prejudicial to the State, to have communicated to another person a document which was calculated to be, or might be, or was intended to be, directly or indirectly useful to an enemy.' You can hardly draw the net more widely, or more unjustly, than that. It is not surprising that he was convicted. All too often, as a Conservative MP has forcefully pointed out, the Acts are invoked in an attempt to cloak official incompetence. On a connected matter, Douglas-Home's extremely crude handling of the affair of the 105 Soviet 'spies' led us straight into the political trap of revealing to both the Russian communist and Western sides that it was Britain more than any other power that was cool over *détente* in Europe.

As a result of recent stupid government action taken under section 2 of the Official Security Act of 1911 a committee has been set up under the chairmanship of Lord Franks, a good former ambassador to the US, and including a successor there in the shape of Sir Patrick Dean, who was formerly chairman of the JIC, to examine that section. Now everyone must agree that an anti-espionage act is essential. But it stands to reason that a wide and vague act which was passed by Parliament on the nod sixty-one years ago, when every dachshund was suspected of being a spy, cannot possibly be appropriate today. Moreover, section 2 refers to 'official information' and leaves it to the officials themselves and to the attorney-general of the day, who is of course a party political appointment, to decide what that blanket term comprises. We must hope that the Franks Committee comes down in favour of abolishing section 2 altogether. The US government, after all, has always managed well enough without any such instrument.[1]

[1] Unfortunately the Committee has recommended a new form of section 2. The Whitehall mandarins think it ought to be even stronger than the old. Journalists and others would like it abolished altogether. We shall see.

ENTERTAINMENT AND PROTOCOL

In a different part of the spectrum are the questions of official entertainment and, connected with it, protocol. I think it is fair to say that in many posts abroad there is far too much of both. The constant round of cocktail parties, lunches and dinners is wasteful of money and time, and hard on the digestion, feet and even brain. These parties do not produce an economic return in information or in the improvement of relations. Indeed they can have the opposite effect: after meeting the same colleagues and their wives a dozen times in, say, a month, it is very possible that a diplomat may feel bored stiff with them. Again, if done at all, grand parties should be designed with care. When Maurice Schumann, the French Foreign Minister, visited London in 1972 Sir Alec Douglas-Home gave a banquet for sixty-six people which included only seven Frenchmen. As a result, the influential members of the French delegation who were only invited to a reception afterwards declined to attend. More to the point would be increased allowances to enable some of our younger and more active diplomats to have more informal social contacts with colleagues, journalists and others who might provide useful information. As for protocol, this should be used strictly to oil the wheels of the diplomatic machine, and not for any pompous or merely traditional purpose. A good many observers of the Queen's visit to France, for instance, considered that valuable opportunities were missed through excessive concern for protocol. Again, in the days when there were a dozen diplomatic missions in a capital it was reasonable to expect every new head of mission to call on all the others, and even for the calls to be returned. But today, when the number of embassies may well be fifty or even a hundred, this custom is a ridiculous waste of time. It would be no bad thing for the United Nations to appoint a committee to examine all such matters with the object of securing general agreement to modernization and streamlining.

WORLD DIPLOMATIC PROSPECTS

To move to higher things, it is certainly a fact that 1971 and 1972 have seen an unusual number of basic changes in the world scene—many of them for the better—and hence of challenges to the world's diplomats and statesmen. At the top of the list, SALT not only remains in being but also makes decided progress. A modernized type of hot-line, via satellite, has been agreed between the US and the USSR with the object of avoiding a nuclear attack by either of them based on some misinterpretation of intelligence received, and of limiting the scope of one should it most unfortunately occur. So the possibility of the world being put at risk by some Finnish peasant getting his mattock into the vital international cable seems to have been removed. Then President Nixon became the first US President to visit China and the Soviet Union, with substantial success in both cases. But the follow-ups will have to be handled with truly Kissingerian adroitness.

Next, the People's Republic of China has been awarded her rightful place in the United Nations; and what is more, and what might not have been the case two or three years ago, she has accepted with alacrity. She must now, by right, be brought into full consultation and participation in the most urgent diplomatic problems, such as disarmament questions and perhaps the Middle East; the main difficulty will be in persuading her to collaborate with the USSR. I must say in passing that I find the complete expulsion of Taiwan, even from the General Assembly, regrettable both on its merits and as a precedent. No doubt communist China would not have accepted membership without this exclusion, so that politically the game is worth the candle. But on the merits of the case Taiwan is just as much a 'peace-loving state', to quote the UN charter, as most, and more so than many; and it is highly probable that she will remain so, independently of mainland China, for a long time. The 'two Chinas' objection has little substance: there have, as we noted earlier, from the start been four Russias in the General Assembly, and there are two Irelands in the shape of the UK and the Republic. But perhaps more serious is the precedent for the future. The UN really does need to include two Germanies, indeed eventually three when West Berlin is made independent, two Vietnams, and two Koreas; but with both the US and China now in a position to wield the veto the alternative, for a very long time, could be none of these. Since, in particular, West and East Germany are among the most powerful industrial nations in the world, this makes a considerable mockery of the universality of the UN.

The US Senate's immediate and peevish decision, following the expulsion of Taiwan, to revoke all aid to countries which need it, was another ominous sign of the widespread resentment of the UN in the US. The damage has been repaired to some extent by the US administration. But it would be foolish to expect China's membership of the UN to lead to sweetness and light all round. The likelihood is that China will use her new forum to step up the propagation of Maoism in the third and fourth worlds. This makes President Nixon's bold and praiseworthy initiative in visiting China all the more important.

The next most significant diplomatic initiatives of recent months have been the various stages of Chancellor Willy Brandt's Ostpolitik, the latest being the first-ever bilateral treaty between the two Germanies. Never has a Nobel Peace Prize been more justifiably bestowed. Finally, Britain's entry into the EEC, now that the final stages have been negotiated, could prove to be of world significance. I only say could, because as of now I am not confident that western Europe is sufficiently united in any way to stand up independently to the US and her sphere of influence, the USSR and hers, China and hers, or Japan and hers. Time will tell, but there is no question that such should be our aim.

That is the world scene in 1972. What, then, is the final purpose of the new diplomacy, with its elaborate apparatus? More vitally than ever, it remains the same as before: peace. Peace on earth, peace below the oceans' surfaces, peace in space. In the case of the super-powers, we should applaud the efforts of President Nixon, of the Soviet leadership, and of the troubled top cadres in China. Britain, as one of the next category of major powers, seems to have lost will and initiative in a cause which is at least as important to her, fundamentally, as to any country in the world. She cannot be rejuvenated by her diplomacy alone, as that is always a function of, and dependent on, a country's economic achievement and morale in general. A substantial move in the right direction would be for Britain to give up various huge items of expenditure which we simply cannot afford: defence expenditure at its present level, and the Concorde, spring to mind. It ought to go without saying that we should firmly remain out of space; but the point must be mentioned because certain US interests are trying to lure certain mindless British prestige-seekers into this vastly expensive sphere. At the same time we could and should give a lead in slowing down the disgraceful—and dangerous—supply of arms to the smaller and underdeveloped countries. In this particular connection it would be honourable, and diplomatically fruitful in the longer run, to forego commercial profit.

Britain's diplomacy can also serve the great cause by backing the United Nations, by supplying aid more generously to the third and fourth worlds, by behaving sensibly in Africa and Asia in all respects, by helping to strengthen the Common Market, and by actively backing the West German government's initiatives for *detente* and security in Europe, instead of hesitating as she has done so far. In the realm of diplomacy as a whole, it calls for men, women and ideas sufficiently fast-moving to keep ahead not merely of today, but of tomorrow and the day after that. Nobody can claim that British diplomacy, or come to that diplomacy as a whole, was markedly successful in the first seventy years of the twentieth century. It has an opportunity to improve on its record in the next thirty years. If it fails, it is liable to become redundant, together with a sizeable portion of the human race.

Postscript

In the six months since July 1972, when I finished writing the body of this book, a gratifying series of favourable developments has occurred on the international scene. It has been possible to incorporate comments on them while correcting the proofs, but it is perhaps worth mentioning them here in a little more detail.

The Vietnam peace treaty has been signed. This entailed two widely differing techniques of the new diplomacy. On the one hand was the heaviest air bombing in the history of warfare, to bring Hanoi to heel. On the other were meetings between Kissinger and the other side, often in shirtsleeves, in small villas in the suburbs of Paris. (One curious by-product was the formalization of the already existing international recognition of two governments of South Vietnam.) No sooner was the peace signed than Hanoi cordially invited Kissinger to come and see the rubble. He accepted with alacrity. We shall yet see Nixon in Hanoi; and perhaps in Havana too, as a result of the United States and Cuba moving closer together over hijacking.

The Security Conference of thirty-four nations, members of NATO, the Warsaw Pact and also neutrals, has got into its stride. The discussions on Mutual and Balanced Force Reductions (MBFR) in Europe between the two alliances in Europe have begun. SALT continues to make progress. Britain has joined the EEC, and now has the opportunity to play a proper part in the world once more. East Germany has been, or is about to be, recognized by numerous Western nations, including Britain. In the Middle East the cease-fire has continued; and it is reported, surprisingly enough in view of Kissinger's origins, that the Arabs would accept him as a go-between. If he can achieve as much for peace there as he has achieved elsewhere, that would indeed be a triumph for the new diplomacy.

Grades and Salaries

To my mind the significance of the figures given below is as follows: (a) they illustrate the appalling rate of inflation in the last few years; (b) nevertheless, the increases in the emoluments of the top ranks have been astonishingly great percentagewise: some trade unions might have a comment or two to make, though the increases obtained parliamentary approval on the trot; (c) although the FCO is one of the UK's most important nationalized industries its top officials receive appreciably less than those of other nationalized institutions, and of course infinitely less than the leaders of innumerable private enterprises.

		1.1.66	1.1.69	1.7.72
Grade 1		£8,600	£8,600	£15,750
Grade 2		£6,300	£6,300	£10,500
Grade 3		£5,335	£5,625	£8,250
Grade 4A		£3,585–4,585	£3,975–5,075	£5,175–6,475
Grade 4E		£4,085	£4,525–5,075	—
Grade 5A		£2,335–3,192	£2,600–3,550	£3,653–4,883
Grade 5E		£2,656–3,084	£2,985–3,525	—
Grade 6		£2,062–2,496	£2,345–2,845	£3,144–3,813
Grade 7A		£1,829–2,240	£2,050–2,479	£2,772–3,488
Grade 7E		£1,659–1,959	£1,865–2,225	£2,476–2,984
Grade 8		£1,011–1,659	£1,145–1,865	£1,530–2,325
Grade 9	Age 18	£633	£775	£1,035
	25	£1,040	£1,225	£1,626
	max.	£1,532	£1,735	£2,325
Grade 10	Age 16	£411	£525	£720
	25	£815	£995	£1,576
	max.	£1,077	£1,225	£1,664

APPENDIX 2

International organizations

I append a list of those major international organizations, together with their abbreviated titles, which are considered 'respectable' by the nations of the three worlds today. Of course they vary enormously in effectiveness and utility.

For the 'un-respectable' organizations of the fourth world who will represent some of the toughest diplomatic problems of the next decades, please see chapter 4.

AID	Agency for International Development (US government agency)
ALALC	Latin American Free Trade Association
ANZUK	Defence pact between Australia, New Zealand, Malaysia, Singapore and the UK
ANZUS	Defence pact between Australia, New Zealand and the United States
ASEAN	Association of South-East Asian Nations
BIS	Bank of International Settlements
CARIFTA	Caribbean Free Trade Association
CCTA	Commission for Technical Co-operation in Africa south of the Sahara
CDC	Commonwealth Development Corporation (UK government agency)
CENTO	Central Treaty Organization
CEPAL	Economic Commission for Latin America
CERN	European Council for Nuclear Research
CMEA (COMECON)	Council of Mutual Economic Aid
EAEC	European Atomic Energy Community (EURATOM)
ECA	Economic Commission for Africa (UN)
ECAC	European Civil Aviation Conference
ECAFE	Economic Commission for Asia and Far East (UN)
ECE	Economic Commission for Europe (UN)
ECLA	Economic Commission for Latin America (UN)
ECOSOC	Economic and Social Council (UN)
ECSC	European Coal and Steel Community
EDF	European Development Fund (EEC)
EEC	European Economic Community ('Common Market')
EFTA	European Free Trade Association

EIB	European Investment Bank (EEC)
ELDO	European Launcher Development Organization
EMA	European Monetary Agreement (formerly European Payments Union (EPU))
ENEA	European Nuclear Energy Agency (OECD)
ESRO	European Space Research Organization
EURATOM	European Atomic Energy Community
FAO	Food and Agriculture Organization (UN)
GATT	General Agreement on Tariffs and Trade
IADB	Inter-American Development Bank
IAEA	International Atomic Energy Agency
IATA	International Air Transport Association
IBRD	International Bank for Reconstruction and Development
ICAO	International Civil Aviation Organization
ICFTU	International Confederation of Free Trade Unions
ICJ	International Court of Justice
IDA	International Development Association (IBRD)
IFC	International Finance Corporation
ILO	International Labour Organization
IMCO	Intergovernmental Maritime Consultative Organization
IMF	International Monetary Fund (IBRD)
ITU	International Telecommunications Union
LAFTA	Latin America Free Trade Association
MCCA	Central American Common Market
NAFTA	North Atlantic Free Trade Area (hypothetical)
NATO	North Atlantic Treaty Organization
NORDEK	Nordic Union (literally Nordic Economic Co-operation)
OAS	Organization of American States
OAU	Organization of African Unity
OCAS	Organization of Central American States
OCAM	Afro-Malagasy Organization
ODECA	Organization of Central American States
OECD	Organization for Economic Co-operation and Development (formerly Organization for European Economic Co-operation (OEEC))
OPEC	Organization of Petroleum Exporting Countries
RCD	Regional Co-operation for Development (Afghanistan, Iran, Pakistan)
SEATO	South-East Asia Treaty Organization
UDEAC	Central African Economic and Customs Union
UEAC	Union of Central African States
UNCTAD	United Nations Conference on Trade and Development
UNDP	United Nations Development Programme

UNESCO	United Nations Educational Scientific and Cultural Organization
UNICEF	United Nations Children's Fund
UNIDO	United Nations Industrial Development Organization
UNRWA	United Nations Relief and Works Agency (for Palestinian refugees in the Near East)
UPU	Universal Postal Union
WEU	Western European Union
WHO	World Health Organization
WMO	World Meteorological Organization
WFTU	World Federation of Trades Unions

APPENDIX 3

The Commonwealth

The Commonwealth consists of twenty-eight full members, plus a few dependent territories. The former are: Australia, Bangladesh, Barbados, Botswana, Canada, Cyprus, Gambia, Ghana, Guyana, India, Jamaica, Kenya, Lesotho, Malawi, Malaysia, Malta, Mauritius, New Zealand, Nigeria, Sierra Leone, Singapore, Swaziland, Tanzania, Tonga, Trinidad and Tobago, Uganda, the United Kingdom and Zambia.

Bibliography

Ball, George W., *The Discipline of Power*, The Bodley Head, London, 1968.

Barnet, Richard J., *The Economy of Death*, Atheneum, New York, 1969.

Clarke, Robin, *The Science of War and Peace*, Jonathan Cape, London, 1971.

Cooper, Chester L., *The Lost Crusade*, MacGibbon & Kee, London, 1971.

Copeland, Miles, *The Game of Nations*, Weidenfeld & Nicolson, London, 1969.

The Diplomatic Service List, HMSO, London, annual.

Diplomatic Service Regulations, FCO, London, current.

Drenker, Alexander, *Diplomaten ohne Nimbus!*, Atlantis Verlag, Zürich, 1971.

Duncan, Sir Val (Chairman), *Report of the Review Committee on Overseas Representation*, HMSO, London, 1969.

Feltham, R. G., *Diplomatic Handbook*, Longman, London, 1970.

Fulbright, Senator J. William, *The Arrogance of Power*, Jonathan Cape, London, 1967.

Fulton, John (Chairman), *Committee on the Civil Service*, HMSO, London, 1966.

Galbraith, J. K., *Ambassador's Journal*, Hamish Hamilton, London, 1969.

Hayter, Sir William, *The Kremlin and the Embassy*, Hodder & Stoughton, London, 1966.

Russia and the World, Secker & Warburg, London, 1970.

Kahn, Herman, *On Thermo-nuclear War*, Weidenfeld & Nicolson, London, 1960.

Thinking about the Unthinkable, Weidenfeld & Nicolson, London, 1962.

On Escalation, Pall Mall Press, London, 1965.

(with Anthony J. Wiener)

The Year 2000, André Deutsch, London, 1967.

The Emerging Japanese Superstate, André Deutsch, London, 1971.

Kennan, George F., *American Diplomacy 1900–1950*, Secker & Warburg, London, 1951.

Russia and the West under Lenin and Stalin, Hutchinson, London, 1961.

Memoirs, Hutchinson, London, 1968.

The London Diplomatic List, HMSO, London, monthly.

Maclean, Donald, *British Foreign Policy since Suez*, Hodder & Stoughton, London, 1970.

Platt, D. C. M., *The Cinderella Service*, Longman, London, 1971.

Plowden, Lord (Chairman), *Report of the Committee on Representational Services Overseas*, HMSO, London, 1964.

Thayer, Charles, *Diplomat*, Michael Joseph, London, 1960.

Trevelyan, Lord, *The Middle East in Revolution*, Macmillan, London, 1970.

Worlds Apart, Macmillan, London, 1971.

Ulbricht, Walter, *Whither Germany?*, Zeit im Bild Publishing House, Dresden, 1967.

Index